IT'S NOT BUSINESS, IT'S PERSONAL

IT'S NOT BUSINESS, IT'S **PERSONAL**

Strategic Conversations for the Next Generation Leaders

RICO PENA

It's Not Business, It's Personal

Strategic Conversations for the Next Generation Leaders

Copyright © 2021 by Rico Pena

Published by: Bexsi Publishing

ISBN-13: 978-1-7378017-0-2

TABLE OF CONTENTS

FOREWORD

As I write these words, we are deep into what some pundits are labeling, "The Great Resignation."

Even as we emerged from a year of shutdowns, lockdowns, mandates, and work-from-home fatigue, and even as we're entering a period of uncertainty with new COVID "variants," people are quitting their jobs in record numbers.

At a time when you'd think people would be clinging to their jobs for security amidst the chaos, four million people quit their jobs in April 2021 alone.

Much has been written about the lower-wage labor shortages, with workers opting for 'stimulus' checks over returning to their jobs in restaurants and hotels; but what about the higher-wage, 'white-collar' jobs?

The answer can be summed up in one word: people.

People respond to incentives, and depending on the time and circumstances, those incentives might be monetary or otherwise.

While the labor shortages among lower-wage workers might reflect monetary incentives, the shortages and resignations at the higher end of the pay scale reflect something very different.

A friend recently told me her husband is looking for a new job, not because he dislikes his current one (he loves it), but because he can't stand the idea of returning to the office after a year-plus of work-from-home. The commute. The wasted time. The time away from his wife.

Incentives matter, and people are being incentivized by things other than pay.

Sixty-four percent of American workers would pass up a $30,000 raise if it meant they had to return to the office and give up their work-from-home status, according to a May 2021 survey by job networking app, Blind. The survey asked 3,000 employees if they'd prefer to permanently work from home rather than get a $30,000-a-year raise. These are employees from companies including Apple, Amazon, Microsoft, Google, Facebook, Goldman Sachs, and JPMorgan.

The purpose of this foreword isn't to debate work-from-home versus office, it's to highlight the main thrust of this book: people.

In Chapter 10, Rico discusses the U.S. company, Gravity Payments, in the context of Maslow's hierarchy of needs. The CEO of the company, Dan Price, lowered his salary and enacted a $70,000 minimum salary for all of the company's employees. As Rico explains, the Price's move helped employees become more fulfilled by removing uncertainty from their lives.

The two basic 'need' tiers of Maslow's hierarchy are physiological and safety needs. By taking care of those needs, Price allowed his employees to focus on the higher tiers, which are love and belonging, esteem, and self-actualization.

What "The Great Resignation" is teaching us is that people are willing to pass up increases in pay (and, perhaps, take pay cuts) as long as their basic needs are met, so that they can focus on the other needs.

After all, after a year of working-from-home, learning to become more self-reflective, and spending more time with their loved ones, people have discovered—or re-discovered—their higher needs.

Those higher needs have, in essence, become incentives that are at least as important as the security of money.

Yes, this is a different world from the one we've been operating for the past century (or more). COVID has changed the game.

Monetary incentives aren't unimportant, but, as one mentor told me years ago, "people are funny."

They were given a year to re-introduce themselves to family, learn what it's like to live without a commute, and have some more freedom in their lives. They adapted to what some called the 'new normal' and now employers and managers are going to have to adapt.

This isn't some 'touchy-feely' call to action, it's simply a reflection of reality.

Culture matters. How you treat the people on your team matters. Each member of your team is a unique individual with a unique behavior style.

As I tell my clients, it's absolutely vital for you to double-down on your awareness and appreciation of your team members' behavior styles, as well as your own, so you can align them to create a truly engaged team of superheroes.

We've moved past the era of having 'people and engagement' trainings as simply an annual nice-to-have-check-the-box exercise.

How your people align with one another (and if they stay with your company) determines how they perform and, ultimately, how the company profits.

This book is a wake-up call to CEOs, presidents, and managers to look up from the spreadsheets and become intentional, aware, and appreciative of the unique behavior and communication styles, strengths, and needs of each of their team members.

One of the hallmarks of an effective business leader is knowing the difference between an expense and an investment. Those who can't see the difference suffer from, as Rico writes, a 'fixed mindset.'

Growth-oriented leaders aren't afraid to invest because they know the money spent today will add to their bottom line tomorrow.

Now, more than ever, investments in your people are critical to the survival and bottom line of your enterprise. This book is a guidemap on how to make those investments wisely.

After all, while I was initially dubious of Dan Price's previously-mentioned efforts at Gravity Payments, the number of employees of the company has reportedly doubled, while the value of payments the company processes has gone from $3.8 billion a year to more than $10 billion.

That's not a bad investment.

Rico brings a wealth of knowledge and experience to the table to show not only the theory and psychology at play in building stronger teams—he shares case studies and nitty-gritty examples of how it can and should be done.

Thanks to Rico for writing this book, and thanks to you for reading.

In Abundance,

Curt Mercadante

ACKNOWLEDGMENTS

Writing a book is no easy task. I should know this as this is my second book, and almost 11 years has transpired. I could use the excuse that I was busy, or I really did not have anything to say. But that would not be accurate. If it wasn't for the support of many people and the belief they had in me I am not sure if this book would have seen the light of day. It is because of them that I am able to present to you, my reader, the book you now hold.

Doug and Jen and their team—they are my publisher, editors, sounding boards, and a group of perfectionist. Thank you for your patience, superior professionalism, for dreaming with me and always keeping us on track. I could not have asked for a better team to Shepheard the ideas (and there were many) from my head into the page.

To all my loyal clients, especially Edgar, Veronica, Trey, Doug, and Jevon, who endured my constant questioning, surveys and, at times, what I am sure felt like an interrogation, A BIG THANK YOU for your support, insights, and candid responses. Much of the book insights came from your honesty.

To my kids Alex and Becca who always provided me with great insights, directions and ideas from the young generation. Thank you for your guidance in making the book relevant to the new generation of leaders.

There is one person above all who deserves much of the credit of this book even being a though in my mind. Like a woodpecker pecking on a hard oak tree, she relentlessly, yet lovingly, pushed, motivated, inspired, suggested, and even provided ideas to writing a second book.

That is my wife Andi. Thank you LOVE for never giving up, always believing in me, and through my stubborn and frustrating times, never giving up. As always, YOU WERE RIGHT!!!

"Success is stumbling from failure to failure with no loss of enthusiasm."

—Winston S. Churchill

IT'S NOT BUSINESS, IT'S PERSONAL

Strategic Conversations for the Next Generation Leaders

An interactive experience

The QR code has been around since 1994. Left to be forgotten in history until a pandemic resurrected it from the dusty halls of the Smithsonian, I wanted this book to be more interactive and fun for my readers. So, I embedded QR codes throughout the book to provide you with an interactive experience in different chapters. Some of the QR codes will open to videos that will provide a visual and more in-depth explanation; some, a podcast or audio; and others, downloadable pdf, ebooks, and work sheets.

Others will provide hidden goodies as my gift to you.

I hope you enjoy the new experience. Please leave me a review on Amazon and share your thoughts on this new immersive experience. I would really love to hear any suggestions or comments. You can email those at CONTACT@THEPOWERTOADAPT.COM

Thank you for reading my book. I hope it brings value and clarity for you.

Rico Peña

"*When you focus on your past, that's your ego.
When you focus on your future, that's your pride.
When you focus on the present, that's humility.*"

—GIANNIS ANTETOKOUNMPO

PREFACE

In every company I have worked with, new leaders, like you, are expected to come fully equipped to lead on day one. You were the very best in your department, and you got promoted but were never given any instruction on how to be a leader. Naturally, you tried to get everyone else to do what you did, to follow the same path that led to your success. You held your team accountable for those actions without recognizing they're not identical people. The same things that worked for you as a new leader won't necessarily work for your team. The same skills that got you the promotion won't necessarily help you in your new position. That was when I decided to write a second book to address the concept of mastering the mindset game of leadership in business as it relates to the human element in every organization.

Maybe you're a younger professional who is trying to manage more senior staff. You have to earn respect. You have to bring the previous generations around to recognize that the mindset, the trends, the market, and the tools have all changed. Experience is valuable, but it is up to the next generation of leaders, the GenXers, the Xennials, and the Millennials to establish the goals and the vision. Each person comes with their own unique experiences. It's how you translate that experience into being a mentor that will enable you to effectively lead your team. I'm here to help you take your skills and translate them into an ability to manage people and bring value to your department or company.

INTRODUCTION

MY PERSONAL STORY

My parents were the greatest influence in my life. My father started his career as a janitor at IBM and retired as a VP. When I asked him about it, he said, "I wanted to do better for myself and for my family. I couldn't do that as a janitor, but if I could get in the door and prove myself, then I knew I could go far." He always told me to set my sights high and prepare for success.

He went in as a janitor and cleaned floors for nine months. Not content to stay there, he befriended one of the people at the next rung on the corporate ladder, an entry-level technician. My father would come in to work a couple hours early every day, sit down with his friend, and learn the position. It was a mutually beneficial relationship. My father received free training, and the friend got some insights and help.

When a position came up at that level, my father had an advocate who talked to the boss. "Listen, he already knows what to do. He's been doing it for seven months."

My father was in the Air Force, an MP in Vietnam. I followed in his footsteps, enlisting in the Marines right out of high school. I served in Desert Storm and Somalia, experiencing things that caused a severe bout of PTSD. My wife was a big help when I came home, and work has always been something that can take my focus away from my personal problems. My father may have struggled with his own combat experiences, though they never stopped him from advancing in his career.

When I was two, he was transferred back to Puerto Rico, which is where our family is from. When he got the job at IBM, we came to Georgia. I was around thirteen years old. The CEO of IBM had been watching his progression and pulled him into the executive branch. He gave my father a couple of books and insights and said, "When you feel like you are ready to pass the mantle on, or if you retire, return these books to me or give them to the next rising star."

That's what he did when he retired in his sixties. My father had an amazing work ethic, and it came from *his* father. My grandfather owned four grocery stores, two bars, and other real estate in Puerto Rico. So, my work ethic came from that, but my entrepreneurial side came from my mom.

My mother has always been an entrepreneur. In Puerto Rico, when I was growing up, my mom had a van, and she would go to schools and sell cakes and empanadas. Instead of an ice cream truck, she drove a home-cooked pastry van. This was before food trucks were popular. In addition, we always had a restaurant or something from the house. She was constantly doing something to make extra money, and her passion created the entrepreneurial spirit in me.

My first businesses were the typical childhood things. I had the paper routes and the grass cutting hustle. But what I think made me a little bit different was that I showed leadership initiative early on. My friends always wanted to make money, but they didn't have the entrepreneurial mindset. So, I said, "Fine, I'll get the jobs. You guys do the work and we'll split the money." I had a crew of young workers mowing lawns across the neighborhood and all I had to do was acquire customers.

My father was always telling me, "If you want it, figure out how you're gonna pay for it. Cause I'm only giving you a house, food, and clothes until you're an adult."

So, there was my training. One day, when I was seventeen, I was washing my dad's car, and I wondered who else would pay me to wash their car. Our neighbor really loved the job I did with my dad's car, and he asked me to detail all these beautiful Corvettes and Harleys he had. I decided, then and there, that I was going to start a new business.

This was before there were carwashes at every gas station. I got a friend on board, and we decided which neighborhoods to target. We wanted customers with high-end vehicles who would pay real money to have them polished and shined. We settled on Buckhead, which is in Atlanta and has all kinds of money. Our next challenge was how to approach the homeowners. We bought khaki shorts and had white polos stitched with the name *Prestige Car Care, Excellence in Motion*. We had some professional trifolds to hand out. We put all the gear in our truck, went to Buckhead, found the biggest development that was not gated, and started knocking on doors.

About three hours later, a gentleman answered our knock and says, "Perfect timing. I've got to go to a wedding in a couple of hours. Can you detail my car?"

"Absolutely," we said, and we started working. We were done in two hours, and the customer was absolutely impressed.

His next-door neighbor saw us working and said, "Can you guys do my Lambo?" Within a weekend, we had the cul-de-sac locked down. Within four weeks, we had half the neighborhood. By nine weeks, I had the entire neighborhood.

No one had ever thought about mobile detailing. By the end of the summer, we were doing so much business, I was thinking, *What am I doing in high school when I can make five grand a week?* Of course, I continued my education, but soon it was a struggle to complete all our work orders on top of our schoolwork. As we were building, I tried to figure out how to manage all our clients. We couldn't keep up with the demand. We were looking at even hiring my lawnmowing buddies again, but we needed guys who knew how to detail specialized cars.

Just when my business had reached its peak of growth, another mobile detailing service from Florida bought us out. We had a great brand name and a reputation for working on high-end cars. We made a pretty penny, and I put all that money into a fund for future investments. The guy who bought Prestige Car Care ended up detailing the executive employees' cars for the 1996 summer Olympics. Because of our brand and the market that we had, we opened doors for him to expand even further. That was my first click into true business. I still have the briefcase and the trifolds that we used.

After finishing high school and returning from service, I continued my entrepreneurial streak. My wife and I created *Fun Times Limited,* which we marketed to summer camps and day care centers. At Fun Times, we would take care of all the logistics of an excursion, to a museum or a pool or a water park. We would handle admission, transportation, food, whatever was needed to provide a day's activity for a group of children. That led into the fitness world. My wife owned a martial arts studio, so we combined the martial arts and overall fitness to train professional and collegiate athletes. Eventually, the different scenarios led us to real estate.

Then came 2008. The housing bubble burst and my wife and I, who were heavily invested in real estate, lost our life savings. We had rentals and homes that lost all their value. The house we were living in, my wife's home, was where our children were born. We had to sell everything in the home; televisions, furniture, jewelry, and everything we could get our hands on just to save the house. We lost all our investments and the money just dried up. We were literally living with a bed and a lamp. My wife's car got repossessed, but I wasn't there to see it. She loved that car, and it was heartbreaking to know that she had watched it towed away. We had to file for bankruptcy. I lost everything. We were two weeks away from foreclosure, and my wife was fighting to keep the house.

I realized then that I would have to swallow my pride and go to work for someone else. I had no car and no money. I had been a sous chef in high school, and I thought, *The kitchen is the only thing I know.* There was a restaurant down the block that needed a prep chef. I talked my way in and worked overtime to pay the bills. I always busted my tail to be the best and started managing that department. I ran the restaurant by the time I was done.

My wife supported me in so many ways. She knew that if I could just get back into the entrepreneurial game, I could make even more money than before. She took a job two hours away, commuting four hours back and forth to support me.

I got a phone call from a friend of mine who owned the top sales training company in the nation. He said, "I have this huge gig with a global company and it's bilingual." He was going to do the English, but he needed someone to do the Spanish. I hadn't spoken Spanish since high school; I didn't even use it in the military. Getting a job in that restaurant, all the other employees spoke Spanish. Mine was really rusty going back into the kitchen, but it gave me an opportunity to practice which turned out to be a lifesaver.

I learned to be agile and moved the needle on my own personal battle plan. I would work in the restaurant from 4:00 a.m. to 1:00 p.m. As soon as this opportunity came, I was speaking and training every weekend for three months. This allowed me to kick-start my business and quit the kitchen.

And it's amazing how things work out. The challenges that I faced gave me an understanding of the struggles that every new leader goes through—how to grow your career, manage a new team, and meet high expectations. These are all priorities. My personal journey led directly to the development of the *Strategies for Peak Performance*. I want to help you overcome obstacles and be as successful in your career as I have been in mine.

WHO THE HELL ARE YOU?

What do I have to teach you that a thousand other coaches don't have? I have been in your shoes. I know what it is like to be promoted because of my skill set and not have any training to manage other people. You realize in that moment that your new position requires more than just the skill that got you recognized and promoted. You see the effect your choices have on the people who you are now responsible for.

This was never so critical as my time in the Marine Corps when I was responsible for twelve lives in addition to my own. If I failed, children would lose parents, parents would lose children, and my team members would die. Those kinds of stakes help you realize the importance of a team. So many of my clients today struggle with the same challenges regardless of company, country, or culture.

How to have difficult conversations, how to motivate, how to communicate as a leader, and how to manage the weight of responsibility are all things no one has taught you. Not many companies are aware of the need for management training for their top performers. Inevitably, this lack of support leads newly promoted managers to quit or perform below their abilities.

I know what that feels like. This is why I developed a tried and true, real-world process that helps the new generation of leaders to be prepared for their next position and to thrive in it. It is one thing to know what to do, it is another to know how to do it.

I have proprietary tools that I use to assess the personality and behavior patterns of new leaders. These assessments are based on brainwave technology and science. They are seven to twelve layers deep, meaning that they go beyond the typical introvert/extrovert data points. We can do seven different types and stack them to give clients actionable intel regarding how they are perceived in the workplace. The common ones that we use are observable behaviors, the way you stand, and the way you hold your hands; all of these communicate just as loudly as your voice.

Team members will pick up on your motivations, your values, and your energy level. They will react to you in ways that you're not even aware of. Some leaders are more about getting things done; some focus on relationships. How do each of these styles function in a team? By helping new leaders understand themselves and others, I can boost team productivity, product development, and connection with the customer. Leaders are instrumental in creating company culture through their motivational techniques and hiring practices. What kind of culture have you created and is your leadership in alignment with your vision and values?

A lot of people have leadership styles that are diametrically opposed to the values of the organization. And they have no idea. They might be telling their sales team to focus on establishing customer relationships yet failing to establish trusting relationships with their own staff. The skills are there, the ability is there, and the experience is there. Sometimes they have a great attitude, but at the core, the values don't match. We are all designed by our upbringing. Our experiences, our parents, and our culture are unspoken motivators that create who we are and lead us to decide what we decide. Once you can put labels on those things, you can demystify most of the common problems all businesses experience.

After working with me, my clients are able to ask better questions in the hiring process to see if a potential employee would be in alignment with the corporate culture and the team. We use assessments to get to the bottom of any personality dispute or ineffective department.

I have experience in both starting my own businesses and working for corporate America. As an entrepreneur, selling my services and assessments, I was able to outsell the other national distributors by two hundred and twenty-five percent in the first year. I became the rookie of the year. That led to a position with a sales training group who needed a Spanish facilitator. And that was what made me realize that my unique approach to people was applicable across all industries. I got into companies that I would have normally not been able to and realized that I could hold my own in a room full of CEOs, CFOs, and VPs. My knowledge and experience could help them achieve better things.

It was the human element. It was always the human element, regardless of strategy or tactics or process. What makes all those things work is the human element that is involved. And when we focused on that, we were able to resolve conflicts that had plagued corporations for years. I had companies in diverse industries—for example, vacation rentals, helicopter manufacturing, bottling, and casinos. They would ask me, "What experience do you have in our industry?"

And I would say, "I have none."

"Then how can you help us?" the executives would ask.

"Are you dealing with people? Are the issues you are having people related or technical?" I would ask.

They would say, "People."

I deal in solving the people issues not the technical or product challenges. That's what I do. Let me walk you through some of the problems you're probably having.

1. Your leadership is struggling to increase productivity and employee engagement due to new virtual demands and uncertainty.
2. You are not comfortable having difficult conversations.
3. Some of your sales team members are not comfortable having virtual conversations and wish for the good old days when they could meet with their clients face-to-face.
4. You are seeing a decline in your closing ratios because the clients are now focusing on shorter, more streamlined meetings and your team is struggling to pivot and adapt to the new demands.
5. Team members have changed their priorities and see the value in working from home and want to change their work environment. This in turn is affecting productivity and customer experience.
6. Different generations within your workforce have trouble establishing synergy.

It doesn't matter what product you're selling. It's about people connecting with people. That's what I do. I work with medium-sized to Fortune 500 companies. Across industries, companies grow through seven distinct stages. I've worked with businesses that had ten employees and businesses that had 500 employees, and I've seen the exact same faults. My method of prioritizing the human component of work can help any organization function better both internally and customer-facing.

It goes right back to your onboarding process. I've interviewed hundreds of human resource professionals; I've looked at all the major onboarding systems, and I've discovered information that you need to move your company forward. I'll show you how you can improve your corporate culture to energize your employees. The energy that you put out resonates through your frontline staff to the customers they deal with. By taking a hard look at yourself and the way you manage people, you can increase the bottom line and bridge the gap between where you are and where you want to be.

SCAN ME
You Tube Video
Who is Rico Pena Power To Adapt

WHY I WROTE THIS BOOK

I wrote this book for all the new leaders out there who have just been handed their first real assignment. Odds are that you have the education, the skills, and the charisma to get ahead in your chosen field, but do you have the training? Too often, leaders are promoted because they excelled as salespeople or engineers. But those skills don't always translate into management. They determine your worth by the final number at the end of the quarter.

Most companies don't offer a leadership academy, throwing you off into the deep end and expecting you to effectively manage people who may be decades older than you. Communication between Millennials and Baby Boomers or between GenXers and the newly graduating Generation Z is ripe for misunderstanding.

WHAT YOU WILL GET OUT OF THIS BOOK

I have seen amazing results for the clients I have worked with. They have been able to grow their staff, fix longstanding conflicts, and increase revenue. The solution always comes down to communication. Every issue I've walked into, there is a breakdown, a misunderstanding, or a total lack of communication. The result is that the company becomes mired in confusion and conflict.

I engage their leadership through self-awareness tools and discussions to be more thoughtful in their approach. After several sessions, clients are more aware of what they need to do to get the best out of their staff. They learn to fix the human problems that start at the top of the food chain and filter down to affect the entire organization. Once they are willing to make adjustments, employees and customers see the effort and respond positively. There's a balance; it's a give and take. But who takes that step first? It is the leader's job to extend that olive branch, to admit their mistakes, and begin to listen to the customer. By opening that dialog, you can heal internal conflict and drive value across departments.

Because that's your job as a leader, to make your employees' lives easier. And it's my job to help you do it. When done right, the success rate goes through the roof. Everyone takes ownership when the lines of communication are open.

We all have baggage, whether it's your upbringing or experience; whatever trauma you have suffered that led you to interact with the world the way you do is unique. We all have that mask that we wear to disguise our true feelings because our human nature is to want to fit in. So, we make adjustments, both consciously and subconsciously, to be accepted. Very few people are comfortable as an outlier, even though those are the ones who change the world. Most of us attempt to adapt to a work culture where we spend most of our time. We are going to do what it takes to fit in, and experience stress if that culture demands something that is outside of our nature.

It is in our DNA, this adaptive response. It is evolutionary; if you are part of the tribe, you are safe, you will find a mate, and your bloodline will survive. If you are reading this today, your ancestors were able to accomplish this task. What does that mean for your corporation? A collaborative person working in a competitive environment won't be very productive. They will do their best to present the attributes necessary for inclusion, but they will generate a lot of stress both for themselves and for the team.

I tell my clients, "By the time I leave, you'll be better off than when I walked in. You will have transformed in ways you could never have imagined, or you won't owe me anything, period. We'll address issues of corporate culture, leadership styles, and communication. You need a minimum of two years for any major structural change. If you have been mired in controversy for seven years, I can't fix it in two days. But I can give you some tools and a brief overview of behavioral theory to help you understand where you went wrong."

There's personnel, there's process, there's performance, and there's customer relations. We've got to look at all of that in order to establish a more productive culture. I lay it all out as a plan with milestones and a robust guarantee. I will stay and work with you until you have achieved the results you are looking for, and I won't ask for a single dime more.

Leaders want to improve performance and accountability in order to meet their goals. For most organizations, whether it's sales or manufacturing, the measurement of success is a number. Did we increase net income? Did we close more sales? Did we expand our market share? Employees are too often judged by numbers and not by their success with people. Did this team complete the project? Did this salesperson retain the customer? Did this manager decrease employee turnover? These are more relational indicators of success that are lost.

There are a lot of strategies and methodologies to help you refocus your energy on people instead of numbers. My job is to help you understand the human element of business because without people, every process will fail. I have dozens of stories from companies I have worked with illustrating problems with leadership and communication. You will learn the importance of having the right people in each process and in an environment that is natural to them. By reading and managing your people more successfully, you can create a more enthusiastic team. They will be more creative and higher performing because you've put them in the right situation that naturally allows them to thrive.

While expressing yourself clearly, establishing a productive workplace culture, and setting goals are all important, by far the most influential thing you will do each day is listen. Philosopher and psychiatrist William James said, "Whenever two people meet, there are really six people present. There is each man as he sees himself, each man as the other person sees him, and each man as he really is." There is no way you can bulletproof your communication without listening. No matter what you say, no matter how well-crafted or innocent, the other person will automatically run it through several filters. They will apply past experience, their knowledge of you, and their interpretation of themselves, and hear only parts of what is said, or misinterpret the message entirely.

Your job as a new leader is to learn to listen effectively. Learn to put away your filters, learn to shut out other people in the conversation, and listen to what your employee is saying. This is easier said than done. People don't always say exactly what they mean. They may have hidden motivations, like supporting family members or paying down a student loan. They may not be comfortable in their position but reluctant to bring it up out of fear of losing their job.

To listen effectively, you need a little background in behavioral theory. We're going to cover Maslow's Hierarchy of needs, which is a theory that explains what people need in order of immediacy. A chapter on the five disfunctions will shed light on reasons why relationships break down and what you can do to fix them. We'll talk about how the stages of growth illustrate problems companies face as they expand from start-ups to industry leaders. Perception governs a lot of how we interact with each other, both self-perception and the way we perceive others. And communication is the bottom line. You'll learn how to do it effectively and how it will benefit your organization.

This book will give you all the tools you need to begin to understand the people and the relationships that you manage. You will take a good look at yourself and your leadership style to determine what kind of energy you are giving off and how your employees will react to it. You will learn how to approach conversations with intention to achieve the best results. Building and maintaining a high-performing team will become second nature when you understand behavior and motivation. Let me help you as I have helped so many other Xennials and Millennials bridge the gap between being a star employee and an effective leader.

"**Next generation leadership** is about leading in the most turbulent of times, and successful **next generation leaders** will be masters of change and resilience." **Leadership** in the **next generation** will be about making not one, but many courageous decisions. From all-nighters to bio-breaks, the next generation brings their own culture to the workplace. The work principles are the same, it's just the method of delivery that has changed. Human behavior theory can help anyone at any level of seniority, but it is especially important to those who have just been handed a promotion.

CHAPTER 1:

PERFORMANCE 101

PERCEPTION CREATES CONNECTION: THE CHIROPRACTIC COLLEGE

I want to introduce one of my clients, a large chiropractic school in South Carolina. They are such a great example of so many concepts in this book, that you will be seeing them throughout the different chapters.

When I first met them, this school was in big trouble. They were on the verge of bankruptcy with only about sixty-five students when they had the capacity to hold over eight hundred. They were one of the oldest chiropractic schools in the country with a legacy to protect. The prior leadership had squandered money, so the board fired him and wanted to be intentional about his replacement.

They decided to bring in someone who understood business, not just academia. They found one of the most successful chiropractors in the country—a well-known, charismatic individual—to lead their school. They wanted to grow their business internationally as well as repair the main campus in South Carolina. This person had that kind of knowledge.

They brought him in, and he did what any businessman would do. He analyzed the corporate structure to locate the dead leaves and started to trim them to make the organization more effective. He had to quickly generate revenue without having any funds to spare for the effort.

He knew who I was, so I got a phone call.

"I was just hired to lead this school and they are in a real bad position," he told me. "We're about to lose our accreditation. I can see some places where I can shake things up, but I'm getting a lot of resistance from the faculty. Can you come in and help?"

I started by doing an assessment of all the staff, faculty, and leadership and quickly recognized that there were two entrenched groups. There was the academic group, who felt that what they had to offer students was a solid curriculum and experienced professors. And then there was the executive team, which was more business minded. They were both going in the same direction but had different ideas on how to get there.

When I talked to the CEO, he stressed the need to generate revenue. He had identified redundancies in many different areas and wanted to streamline processes. That work had to be done before attracting students, and yet they needed students if they were going to remain solvent. Their sales team was disseminated, and they needed to hire more people. The roadblock they kept running into was their lack of funds;

they didn't have the money to pay new staff. The new leader was trying to figure out how to cut costs to invest in the future.

The academic camp said, "You're moving too fast." They were panicking over the proposed changes. "This is not how we've done it," they complained. "We've got to protect our legacy." All they had ever done at the school was in danger of changing, and they were digging their heels in.

In behavioral science, you have fast-paced behaviors and reserved behaviors. Those who move at a fast pace like momentum; it means they're getting something done. Those who prefer a reserved pace want to take their time and plan out each step before taking it. In this chiropractic school, the staff consisted of the accounting team, sales, recruiting, operations, faculty, and a working clinic on top of that. We had to completely redesign the culture to get everyone on board. We had to take the fast-paced movers from the executive camp and slow them down so that the reserved academic staff could meet them halfway. It took me three and a half years, but we went from bankruptcy and sixty-five students, to having over five hundred students and a twenty-million-dollar capital investment. They are now the number-one chiropractor school internationally.

Performance can be hindered by a lack of team unity. Just because the teachers were well educated and cared about their students didn't mean that they worked well within the established culture of the school. We had to change the culture to boost productivity and create a message that the entire staff could get behind. The behavioral component to staff management turned out to be the key to boosting performance and rescuing a failing organization. As a new leader, you need to take the time to address underlying conflict before you will be able to see results from your team.

HIGH-PERFORMING TEAM

In order to turn the chiropractic school around, its new leader had to mold the staff into a high-performing team. The hidden benefit of higher performance is not only that people are performing better, but that the entity takes on a life of its own. You need less fuel to keep the thing going. Once you get the entire staff dialed in, there's less conflict and more focus, and there's positive momentum that sustains itself. Less energy is wasted so more can be spent on productive activities.

Focus = currency.

In an unproductive team, how many hours are wasted in arguments and by individuals trying to prove that they're right? If you could take just ten percent of that time and apply it to a higher level of performance, what would that equate to at the bottom line? The customer is going to pick up on that discord, even if they are not consciously aware of it. A high-performing team generates a better customer experience simply by being in tune with each other.

One of the flagstones of a high-performing team is that they don't fall apart when any one individual is missing. If someone goes down, someone else can grab the flag and continue the mission. Doc Rivers is a famous basketball coach who led the 2008 Boston Celtics team to a championship using the same approach the military uses. He created a common theme that brought everyone together and held them accountable. Wining the Championship.

In the Marine Corps, we had *esprit de corps*. The mission is first and foremost; the mission must be accomplished above all else. That is what it means to be a Marine. That is why we train as a team and develop the skills, fitness, and mindset that are legendary. To accomplish the mission in the most effective way, as a team, you must understand the Marine way of doing this and to do so you must learn to be a **Marine**.

Doc Rivers leaned into the *esprit de corps*. The team had sixteen titles, and there was an open space in the display case where the seventeenth title would go. He got one of those big movie spotlights from the theater and he had it focused on that empty spot 24/7. This resonates with the Focus formula. Focus creates curency, but focus can only be created by means of *novelty*. The spotlight that was directed at that empty spot aroused a strong sense of desire among everyone in the team to fill that spot with the Celtics banner. The light shining on the space represented their will to win! Doc Rivers also created this internal thing called *ubuntu*, which is an African term that loosely translates into "one for all." But what was brilliant about this strategy was how he presented it to the team. He got all the rookies together to explain the methodology, something they never had to do before. This approach, like the spotlight at an empty spot, created novelty. Novelty played a huge role in boosting the team's spirit that led to their winning the championship. The space where the spotlight was focused now hangs the 17th banner!

"Now," he said. "I want you guys to present it to the senior players. It's up to you to make sure they understand why it's important."

Novelty = Focus

Focus creates currency.

Because it came from team members, not from the coach, it was adopted, and it became the fabric of the team. He had a funny story to illustrate how well the concept worked. He was getting on a plane to go to an away game, and he had a burger. The team chastised him. They said, "That's not good *ubuntu*. Where's our burgers?" They weren't fooling around. They had internalized the "one for all" mentality and they used it to help propel them to victory and win that seventeenth title.

In the Marine Corps, if our staff sergeant had said, "This is what we're doing," we would have followed orders, but it doesn't mean we would have liked it. When direction comes from teammates that we shared blood, sweat, and tears with, that was a whole different story. The buy-in is elevated. People are more open, and they can articulate the solution from their point of view. Momentum comes from the team itself, not from an outside leader or established authority figure. As a new manager, there will be times when you will have to intervene in your team's process but figuring out how to minimize or disguise your influence will boost your team's performance.

Serena Williams' tennis coach said, "Our job isn't to teach athletes how to play the sport. Our job as coaches is to remind them of the champions they already are." If you hire the very best, they know what they do. They already have that entrepreneurial mindset; they just need to know where they're supposed to stand and how they are being measured.

Leaders who run high-performance teams have learned to prepare their teams for changes in the environment by communicating the What, Why, and When. Once you have established a team that works well together, they are more adaptable to change than a fractured staff. Change can come from anywhere: a new team member, a new product, or a natural disaster that affects the supply chain. High-performance teams can adapt well to new situations when their leaders communicate openly and honestly. You can ask for feedback from the team as to how best to implement the changes in a way that will not disrupt the routine but rather enhance it. The ultimate goal of any new leader is to help their people grow and exceed their expectations of themselves while guiding each one of them to work together as a high-performing team.

HOW PERFORMANCE IS DEFINED

There are three basic ways that performance is defined:

1. **Justifiable or measurable results**
   There is a problem that the team can solve, and there's a methodology or solution to apply to it. It's very tactical. In the military, the justifiable or measurable result is whether the mission has been achieved. Leaders painstakingly explain the mission, the objectives, and the roles so the team has no questions. Everyone knows where they fit into the execution of that singular mission. Because when things go south, and they do, it's

the focus on the outcome that allows people to course correct and still get the mission done.

2. **How a team functions together**

What does a cohesive team look like in your culture, product, or service? If being cohesive yields a good performance, what's keeping your team from achieving the best results? Is it you? Is it the environment? Did you hire the wrong people? When we dig deep to discover why people act the way they do, we uncover the core. Why do you think military special forces have a selection process? To weed out the ones who do not have the right character and the mental, physical, and emotional stability to endure the challenges the job calls for.

Ineffective leadership can hold people back from achieving their highest level of performance, both culturally and individually. If you put two people together who have different behavioral styles, motivations, or value systems, they might not function well. An external crisis such as the pandemic or a market fluctuation might cause stress that impacts the team's ability to do its job. It may take some detective work to determine which factor is preventing your team from achieving its best results. Clarity of communication is your best bet when trying to boost performance in a struggling team. Most leaders evaluate their teams' and team members' performance based on the financial achievements and goals they have accomplished. They struggle to find the best ways to motivate people to perform at a higher level.

3. **How well an action, product, or process is received by the customers**

   A stage play can be called a "performance," and just like a play, any corporate action needs an audience. Your customers are the ultimate review of whether your processes are working or not. An increase in sales can be taken as measurable success, but an increase in customer retention rate means much more going into the future. A salesperson who performs well is adept at creating relationships with your clients. A product that performs well brings value to the customer's life or solves an unmet need. A team that performs well creates an atmosphere of productivity that extends beyond their meeting room to infect the entire culture of the organization.

WHY DOES PERFORMANCE MATTER?

Performance matters because it empowers people and creates a better quality of life. Nobody wants to be mired in conflict. For many of us, a large portion of our days is spent at work. In fact, the average person will spend 90,000 hours at work over a lifetime.

It's safe to say your job can make a huge impact on your quality of life. No one wants to go to work every day to accomplish nothing with the ultimate reward of bankruptcy. The goal of performance is to increase return on investment, enhance the customer journey, win the title, or publish the bestseller. These things have value for all companies no matter what stage of growth or industry. I think it comes down to the core of this book; performance matters because we are human, and it is written into our DNA.

If we look at the second definition of performance, the one that measures how well our engine works, are you trying to get the most out of people? Are you hiring correctly? Are you taking the current culture into consideration when deciding whether a new hire will be the right fit? Or are you just searching for someone with the right knowledge and skills for the specific opening you have at that moment in time? By taking the team into consideration and choosing a person with compatible behaviors, you can maximize performance and minimize disruptions.

Take a page from an engineering textbook. They look at a problem and determine the desired solution. Then they work in between to test possible solutions to grow and improve the model. If we did this with the human components of our business, instead of remaining locked into the hierarchy, we might improve processes exponentially. Flat companies such as Google and Apple work people in teams with few levels of senior management. Performance then is measured by the value each team brings to the company, and not where the team fits into the vertical structure. Performance matters because it is the ultimate goal of the work we do and the reward for productive team membership.

The new CEO of Ford, Jim Farley, is somewhere between a Baby Boomer and a GenXer. He was born in 1962, and so represents the oldest of the next generation. When Ford was going bankrupt, they hired Farley from Siemens to shake things up. He walked into the conference room with all the senior executives and started asking questions. He **listened**.

And one of the things that he kept hearing was that no one was comfortable talking to Ford himself and letting him know where the problems were. The owner didn't want to hear it. He wanted to think everything was working fine until it was too late.

So, the first thing Farley did was to eliminate that executive space. He created a half moon room, almost like a college type coliseum for each department. Each room had a green light, red light, and yellow light area where projects and processes were discussed. That meant that no one was in charge. The person in the middle of the room, doing their presentation held all the attention until the floor opened for comment. And what that did is that everyone started to see how each department's actions had a ripple effect on the next department, from sales to marketing, to the creation of the vehicle; everything was interconnected.

These round tables, if you will, generated conversation that started to break down the barriers between departments. People were suddenly able to talk about bottlenecks and low hanging fruit. They were able to approach problems first by acknowledging that problems existed. Each department could see how their own processes affected other departments. And then they would go into this room, and they would put all the milestones on a visual task board.

A green light meant "We're on task for our next meeting. We're good." A yellow light meant "Something is off, but it can wait till the next meeting." A red light meant "Stop the presses. We need to have this conversation right now, or it's going to affect everybody else." Anyone could walk into that room and see instantly where each process had stalled and what was performing well. This strategy leveraged communication through partnerships rather than hierarchical structure.

Performance was enhanced by breaking down the barriers to communication and allowing teams to cross pollinate. In the case of Ford, performance brought the company back from the brink of failure. Open communication and a restructuring of the leadership process was what made all the difference.

MEASURING PERFORMANCE

When we measure performance in business, it is typically through numbers and data. In the military, we perform what is called "mission autopsy." In a clinical autopsy, you open things up and you discover the cause of death. We used to call it "bullets and Band-Aids." It was the process of sitting down and evaluating what went right, what went wrong, and how we could apply that knowledge to the next mission. It was a way to measure performance. What was the outcome of the mission and what could we do better? In business, this is called KPI (Key Performance Indicators).

Every team is made up of individuals. Like a Lego wall, the team is only as strong as its links. A typical military mission had a leader, but it might also require a demolition expert. The mission wouldn't be a success without either of those two pieces, and the leader can't function as both. To manage a team, you need to look at every detail that each individual needs to be successful. In the Marine Corps, we looked at security, the terrain, what type of demolition was needed, and what kind of product we were blowing up. Different materials have different fall rates; if you are blowing up a concrete building versus a brick building, you need to know what to expect. You have to examine all these little things to make sure you cover every possible element needed for success. And the leader is in charge of collecting and communicating all this information so that the team members can perform their duties.

The mission is the priority. And bringing our people home was the next priority. So, what do we need to do collectively as a team to achieve those two things? That is the measure of performance. Notoriety, medals, or awards ceremonies, we couldn't care less; it's about working together as a team. But how do you get to that when you are put in charge of a new team? The Marine Corps drills into its personnel: the mission, the mission, the mission, because the mission is greater than any one person. In business, it's about numbers, numbers, numbers, but often at the expense of the individual or the team.

When we look at business performance, we're mostly looking at the bottom line, the profit and loss, or return on investment. These are the metrics by which the health of a business is usually determined. We do not tend to give the same weight to the ability, skill, willingness, desire, and drive of our employees who deliver those numbers. There could be external factors that affect the bottom line but have nothing to do with the effectiveness of the product development team. For example, the distribution network could be damaged by an international incident, disrupting the new product rollout. This delay could artificially depress the numbers, and yet have nothing to do with the innovative new packaging the design team created. Measuring performance based on productivity, achievement, and problem solving may be a better way to get at value than just profit and loss.

Let's not forget the human element of performance. Yes, automation and AI can contribute to overall company profits, but a mission will never be successful without people to run it. The cultural design of financial awareness dictates that you are only successful if you meet certain financial milestones. A lot of improvement programs spend so much time with lower achieving sales representatives that they fail to see the problems in the hiring process. No matter how much training and managing you throw at the problem, you are not going to improve because you've hired the wrong people. And because your top achievers don't cause any headaches and they're always generating money, they don't get the training they may need. You expect your salespeople to bring the human element to the customers to gain those numbers, yet you don't value what they bring to the table as people.

Another way to think about measuring performance, that really gets to that bottom line number, is by value/salary. If you're paying $60,000 a year for a salesperson, what is the return on investment you want for that $60,000? You have margins on your products, but you have no margin of performance for your people. So how can you set standards, expectations, training, KPIs, or outcomes that will motivate your employees to do their best? Most companies don't think the same way about staff as they do about traditional investments. If you're going to invest $60,000, maybe you want that position to generate $1.2 million in the next twelve months. If that is the case, how do you reverse engineer that figure to provide your sales staff with actionable goals that motivate them?

Performance measurements based on numbers isn't a bad thing in itself. After all, at the end of the day, shareholders want to see a profit. There is, however, more at play than the rise and fall of lines on a graph. People are an investment of time and money both for you and for themselves. If managed properly, and teamed up efficiently, they can move the company ahead. The mission is more important than any one individual, and as a leader, it is your job to make sure everyone understands the mission and their role in seeing it through. In addition, you can help them see how the team's mission will help them reach their personal goals. Performance then can be measured based on both how well the team functions and whether or not the mission was a success.

TRAINING

The military spends ninety to ninety-nine percent of their time training for that ten percent of the time when they've got to go into action. In the corporate world, you're acting ninety to ninety-nine percent of the time and training one to ten percent of the time. It's backwards, and the results reflect the inconsistency. Why do the armed services have bootcamp? Anyone can sign up to be a Marine, but you have to go through bootcamp and Marine Corps Recruit Training in order to be selected. In training, a hopeful Marine can expect to confront food rationing and sleep deprivation, day and nighttime marches, combat resupply, and casualty evacuation scenarios, and no-light infiltration movements.

When I look at the onboarding processes of a lot of these companies, they don't have a process to determine whether a new hire can really perform. Often, they don't even have a way of extending expectations at the very beginning. Are they getting any kind of ninety-day coaching with someone else to see if they can perform and meet expectations? Once they're in the system, what is the ongoing training for development?

Most companies would save so much money on the onboarding if the hiring staff gave consideration not just to skills and experience, but also to culture, connection, and the environment their employees will be working in. It could start by adding a personality assessment to their current hiring process and making sure that potential employees match the current culture. This type of assessment should constituent a full third of the hiring process to help narrow down the final candidates.

I'm not talking about screening people out based on legally protected classes such as race, gender, or national origin, but about temperament, motivation, ideal environment, or competitiveness. Then put them through a rigorous training component, not just to increase acumen, but to see if they're still the right person. Can they deliver what they said they would in the interview? And after all the training and onboarding, put them through a ninety-day temporary period from which either of you can walk away gracefully. When this happens, you shorten the learning curve that any new team member has before they can integrate productively into your company.

I worked with one hiring manager who used a quick test as part of the interview process to narrow down the list of candidates. It was a sales job, but it was during the recent 2008 recession, so he had hundreds of applicants, and not all of them qualified. One individual lied her way through the online automated behavioral assessment. She presented herself as more competitive, and more sales oriented than she actually was. In the interview, he asked her to sell him her favorite product. She chose a diet soda and proceeded to list three or four things about diet soda that she enjoyed.

"It has no calories. It tastes good. The can is pretty." Then she stopped. She had no idea how to sell anything, and if the company had relied on just the hiring software and basic interview, they would have wasted both time and money.

I have known many high-level companies that do not have a defined internal career path. They lose top performers because these people, unlike the ineffective sales candidate, can move to another company when they want to grow. That should be part of the onboarding process, to make new employees aware of their options. You may have hired them for the current position, but if they excel, they need to know how to grow in the company and accelerate their career. When they get there, they can choose other plans, and their career can unfold within your organization.

It's the same thing in the military; when you get to a certain point, you've earned the ability to move up. You could have the very best people and they are only performing at fifty percent because you've only given them the ability to stay where they are. When you have the right processes and the right training, you can take someone who maybe has an initial ability of thirty percent and skyrocket them to eighty percent.

CRITICAL THINKING

Critical thinking is an essential skill for every leader and every team. Potential solutions can come from anywhere, and part of effective leadership is being open to suggestions. I have a story about a company I worked with, in which I was able to think outside the box to solve a specific problem.

The company contracted with local hospitals to pick up and wash their linen. The problem was that there were too many hospital personnel trying to keep track of the patients and the linen at the same time. They never knew what they had in stock. The pandemic caused a surge in hospital admissions, and the cycle of replacing linens accelerated. Without a good process in place to begin with, the mechanism began to break down, and the cost of emergency replacement was growing exponentially. We needed a creative solution to keep track of everything.

"I think I have a solution that will solve the problem and make this run much more smoothly," I said to the CEO. "What if we put an RFID chip in each piece of linen and an RFID reader on every cabinet door at the hospital?"

"How would that help?" The owner seemed perplexed, but intrigued.

"If we do that, the hospital will be able to track each piece of linen as it's taken out of the cabinet and will be able to keep closer track of the inventory. They will know what they're using, how much they have left, and when they need to re-stock their supply. But the best part is that they won't have to do anything. The chips and readers will automatically show what is in stock and what needs to be reordered."

The owner thought it over for a moment. "This would make inventory easier on their end as well as ours, wouldn't it?"

The last thing I wanted was for the healthcare workers to have to take time away from caring for patients to support this new system. It needed to work in the background, in a way that the only people actively aware of what was happening were those in the billing department. We contracted with a technology group to make it happen and pitched it to the director of the hospital.

We started implementing the new RFID chip technology in May of 2020 and it has helped the hospital keep track of linen in such an efficient way that they no longer have to deal with it on a daily basis. Best of all, the linen supply company didn't have to rely on a single person at the hospital to figure out when they needed to reorder because the system we put in place automatically alerted them that it was time.

Critical thinking is the beginning and end of effective teamwork. Whether the original suggestion comes to you from a consultant, from a customer, or from an employee, being open to new ideas will enable you to innovate in new ways. As a new leader, one of your jobs is to facilitate the problem-solving process. By following through on suggestions instead of shutting them down, you can enhance the customer experience and drive new value in your market.

PERFORMANCE 101

These are the basic considerations for team performance: how to nurture it, how to enhance it, and how to measure it. You can nurture performance by hiring the right people, putting them together in the right environment, and allowing them to thrive. You can enhance performance by setting clear goals and communicating the mission. Go into detail. The more your team understands about the mission parameters and how their individual role or actions contribute to the success of that mission, the more likely they are to succeed. You can measure performance using data points such as profit and loss and return on investment, but a better way to measure is to combine the numbers with the milestones each team member was able to achieve. People are at the heart of every business, and you need to understand their motivations, ideal environment, and behavior if you are going to encourage them to perform at their best.

CHAPTER 2:

SELF-MASTERY, IT ISN'T THAT HARD TO LEARN

THE IT PROFESSIONAL

A recent client who was in charge of the IT support for a private school had an employee whose specialty was Apple Mac computers. We will call him Steve. The entire school ran off these Apple computers, so they had Steve to fix any issue. He was brilliant and charismatic, but not exactly a team player. To be generous, I'll call him 'exotic.'

Many of the teachers who went to him struggled with either internet connection, forgotten passwords, or difficulty accesing their documents; these were common everyday complaints. The school followed a ticket system to deal with various IT issues. You put in a ticket and wait for your number to come up. If everyone followed the ticket system, Steve would have an ordered list of jobs, and he could go one by one and solve each problem. Sometimes, some of the malfunctions were pervasive and extremely urgent that people would simply come knocking on his door. In an hour, he would have five, six, or eight people come to complain personally and demand that he fix their computers immediately. They were claiming that the issues were keeping them from being able to teach the class, give a test, or just being able to grade exams. Steve lost his temper because it was uncomfortable for him. He didn't like that much personal interaction. It was interfering with his process and workflow.

Once we realized why he was reacting negatively, we sat down with him and started to work on conflict resolution. He was dealing with conflict both within himself and with the particular customer base. We explained to him the reasons for such urgent requests from the faculty as well as the consequences if their computer issues continued to be unresolved for a prolonged period. He admitted that his frustrations were coming from mistakenly thinking that the faculty members were bypassing the process. He also admitted that he never took the time to ask about how the impact of computer issues are affecting the teachers' ability to do their jobs. The testing system was crashing and therefore affecting students' grades, which could also affect the school's revenue and its relationship with the state.

Once Steve understood the gravity of the situation, he started seeing the reasons behind the urgency. He was able to communicate with the teachers more effectively without getting annoyed. He also started a ticket system that will tag a request as high priority as needed. This served as a signal for Steve to prioritize those that urgently needed his attention, bearing in mind the impact earlier described. If Steve's boss and myself had not taken the time to ask questions, we would never have uncovered the source of the problem. We addressed the conflict in a calm, non-confrontational manner, and helped the struggling employee see beyond his own desk. Once we brought him back on board, he was able to contribute to the productivity of the school in a more efficient way. It took 1) great leadership skills to uncover the core issues; and 2) open communication with the employee to develop an understanding and a plan to move forward.

LEADERSHIP

Military high-performance specialist Harry Moffitt explained, "The best new leaders I have observed have what I term a 'Constant Gardener' effect. Rather than seeking to influence, motivate, and direct people, they nurture them like a garden. They use rich soil and safe, favorable environments, to provide everyone room to flourish."

Jim White, the 1987 cross-country coach at McFarland High School in Sweetwater Texas, was made famous by Kevin Costner's film *McFarland, USA*. Based on the true story of a 1987 cross country team from a mainly Latino high school in McFarland, California, the film stars Kevin Costner as Jim White, the school's coach, who leads the team to win a state championship through understanding culture, language, and the willingness to put himself in their shoes to determine their needs and motivation. Despite early failures, he sought out new training opportunities and encouraged each player individually to reach their potential.

When I work with new leaders, I am usually coming in at a crisis point. It is usually when they realize they are human, and they do not know how to lead in the chaos of uncertainty. They are no longer in their wheelhouse, doing what *they* did as an *employee* to succeed. Management requires a whole new skill set, one that they were not taught before they were expected to perform.

Next generation leaders often manage their people simply by instinct or trial and error. If you take a step back and apply some simple principles, like being vulnerable and honest with the team, you can create an amazing level of growth. Small adjustments can generate massive change. What I teach new leaders first is to *over*communicate with their team.

> *Based on my observation, some of the characteristics that define next gen leaders are: relatively young, innovative, nimble, tech-savvy, mission-driven but not at the expense of the team, and focused on communication and balance for work and home; they manage or lead others for the first time, possess a hunger for success, constantly seeking inspiration, and challenge the hierarchy.*

So often, the leader thinks they have disseminated knowledge, but the team still has gaps in their understanding. Have you ever asked someone a question, only to hear the answer, "Didn't you get my email?" As a leader, you can never afford to send a single email and expect everyone to understand mission parameters.

I once had jury duty, and the clerk who was in charge of corralling all of the potential jurors knew her job backwards and forwards. Everything she said to that room of one hundred unhappy people, she said slowly and clearly, and she repeated herself three times.

"You are going to be here until five o'clock. You are going to be here until five o'clock. You are going to be here until five o'clock." It sounds redundant, but none of us had any questions about how long we were going to have to sit in that room.

As a new leader, you need to get together with your team and discuss real options. You need to figure out what they know, what they need to know and what kind of a plan they can construct with that information. The key is to keep moving forward, and to support them in their process so that they can perform at peak effectiveness.

HAVING DIFFICULT CONVERSATIONS

Many of the clients I work with who are new to a leadership position seem to struggle with the same challenges. "How do I have a difficult conversation that does not end up in hurt feelings or anger?" "How do I lead a team that a month ago I was a part of?" "What do I say to a team who has been together for a long time, is older than me, and I am the outsider brought in to lead?" (I get that one *a lot*!!!)

Most often what they are looking for is the magic pill, words, or a specific skill that will fix everything. They soon realize that the simple solution they are looking for does not exist. You have to work at it. There is a simple solution, but it is not easy to recognize, let alone master.

For many of the next generation leaders, the most difficult conversation they will have is with that person they see in the mirror every day. You see, most of the challenges mentioned above are all symptoms of a greater problem—lack of confidence. I don't mean personal confidence; I am sure you have that, or you would not have been able to get to where you are right now. No, I mean the kind of confidence that comes from trial and error, that develops a certain acceptance of your abilities in a specific situation. This type of confidence means you are no longer **unconsciously unaware**, you are **consciously aware** and know exactly what to do and the outcomes you want before you even start.

PDF
EQ E-book

SELF-MASTERY

Many of the successful leaders we look up to have many things in common including this type of confidence that comes from years of self-mastery. It is the kind of confidence that is not afraid of elevating others, encouraging team members, and always being empathetic. They are comfortable with who they are, what they bring to the table, and are not threatened by others' opinions or successes.

This level of confidence stems from having those honest internal conversations that lead to the difficult realizations of your short comings and how your self-preservation ego is leading the way. (More on this in *Chapter 7, Maslow's Hierarchy*). These leaders have the courage to follow a process to course correct, improve their skills set, and elevate their level awareness. This eventually creates the type of leader others are willing to follow even before you say a word.

We call this **self-mastery**. How can you lead anyone to greatness or to expect them to live up to the potential you see in them if you cannot do so for yourself? Just like the scent of body odor after a long muggy day in the Florida sun with no deodorant, that incongruency will hit your team every time, causing them to feel that something just does not add up.

So, what does self-mastery mean? As retired FBI Special Agent, Joe Navarro describes in his latest book, *Be Exceptional,* "Self-Mastery allows for a conscious and honest appraisal of ourselves that can compel and support us to strive and try harder, and to grasp the nuances of awareness that can make the difference between failure and success." This is how you take command of your life through your daily habits and behaviors by focusing on how to build the scaffolding essential to self-mastery and eventually develop yourself into the leader that can make a difference.

Mastery is often equated with skill, and it is not. Skills are the physical actions used on a regular basis to achieve something — building a car, chiseling a statue, or winning a gold medal. However, the ability to maximize a skill that is required to reach your fullest potential is only achieved once you have self-mastery. Think of Michael Phelps, the most decorated

Olympian of all time. To reach that level of success required much more than athletic ability. He demonstrated and honed self-mastery skills such as: focus, dedication, industriousness, curiosity, adaptability, self -awareness, and determination. He was laser focused on the pursuit of his goal. Skills are just one side of the self-mastery coin. You must conquer and develop self-awareness in order to achieve an elite level of leadership.

EMOTIONS AND TEMPER TANTRUMS

The other side of self-mastery includes knowing your emotions, strengths, and, above all, your weaknesses. By understanding honestly who you are at all levels, you will know when you need to let someone else take the lead (despite your ego). This may be the case when the task at hand is just not your thing, or if you're having a bad day and you are not at your best.

The first area we all must master is our emotions; they rule everything we do. The better you are at emotional regulation, the more control you will have of the road to self-mastery. Just like a steering wheel controls the direction of a car, so do our emotions steer our reactions in different environments and situations. At times we are that 16-year-old with a muscle car for the first time and other times we are a Formula One champion racer. They only difference is mastery of skill and self.

Have you ever seen a child throw a temper tantrum in the grocery store because they were not getting their way? I mean full out foot stomping, hand pumping, high pitch whining, crying wrinkled face, throwing themselves on the floor, and spinning around type of temper tantrum? Now think back to that exact moment and focus on how you felt experiencing this event: happy, sad, disgusted, or shocked?

Now ask yourself, why did you feel that way? Remember that answer.

If it was your boss doing that, would you respect them? Have you ever lost your temper, raised your voice, and spoke angrily to others? Did you demand action or were you frustrated that others were not doing what you wanted in the way you would do it? That, my friend, is a temper tantrum. Remember the emotions you felt when you saw the child in the grocery store: your employees are viewing you very much in the same way.

When a leader loses their temper, raises their voice in anger, makes demands, and allows their ego or frustration to dictate their choices, at that very moment they lose the trust, respect, and loyalty of their team. It is replaced with fear and lack of respect. Would you go above and beyond for a leader you don't respect? Can you be at your very best when you are in fear of losing your job? I am going to guess no. Why should anyone follow or respect an adult who throws temper tantrums, who is emotionally out of control, and what they will do next is uncertain? There is nothing like going to work walking on eggshells. Recent studies show that the average time spent with your coworkers and leaders is 90,000 hours per lifetime. That is a very big omelet.

IDENTIFYING YOUR TRIGGERS

So, you may be asking, "How do I even start to build self-mastery?" Like all master communicators, you start by asking the right questions.

> *"You can tell the size of a man by the size of the things that bother him."*
> **—Adlai Stevenson, diplomat**

The key to regulating our emotions is to come to the realization that our emotions, just like a steering wheel in a car, will affect the direction of our choices. The secret is to recognize the triggers that may cause us to lose control. Just like driving and hitting a pothole or seeing debris on the road, how you react determines the level of control or composure you have over that situation. Start by asking yourself some simple questions.

(Get a sheet of paper and write this out. The more honest you are, the better the outcome of this exercise for you. If you are not sure, ask someone whose opinion you trust and who knows you well to give their opinion of your answers to the questions.)

1. What emotions do I find most challenging to manage (worry/fear, sadness, anger, ...etc.)?
2. What situations do I seem to be in when those emotions occur? (meeting, driving, at work, kid's birthday party, ... etc.)?
3. What tends to "set me off" (too many tight deadlines, stupid questions, long work hours, when someone says X or does Y, when a combination of _____)?

4. When my emotions are out of control, how do I tend to behave (yelling, being an asshole to others, bullying, sulking, throwing things, withdraw, self-medicate, eat, over exercise, other_____)?

Once you can clearly see your triggers, you can now start to create strategies to build an immunity towards them. There is an old saying, "If you can name it, you can tame it." Creating a clear and honest awareness of these situations helps you to gain mastery over them. Some great ways to start building counter measures for these triggers are:

1. Think of your trigger situations.
2. Think of people, characters, or mentors who you know or have observed and what they do in these situations. Pick a few and really observe them. Take notes and start to practice some of their actions.
3. Do they take a deep breath before they respond? Do they maintain their cool in high pressure circumstances? Are they respectful even when others around them are not?
4. Seek to replicate their reactions when you find yourself in the same situations.
5. Once you have discovered your triggers, find books, blogs, or YouTube videos on how to manage and master that emotion. Find the ones that resonate the most with you.

Remember, Michael Jordan, Usain Bolt, and Serena Williams achieved success by finding solutions and applying them with dedication and persistence. The goal was not an easy fix, it was mastery of that area of their game that needed to be elevated or fine-tuned.

And if all else fails, ask a person you would like to emulate what they do or how they overcome a specific situation. Once you have a strategy you are comfortable with, find an accountability partner. You need a person in the office that is not afraid to call you out when you are "half-assing it" or being lazy. This person always has your best interest in mind even when you are looking for a shortcut. This will ensure you will succeed in mastering your emotional dial.

TAKING CONTROL OF YOUR EMOTIONS

The best phrase I have ever read that helps me to keep focused is:

> *"Don't wallow, don't whine—take focused, constructive action."*
> **—Joe Navarro from Be Exceptional**

Having control of your emotional dial does not mean you are an ice-cold robot with no emotions like Data from Star Trek who looks at all things from a purely logical and process-minded perspective. Not at all. It is about being in control of how and when those emotions manifest themselves. Leaders who are conscientious about what they do have the ability to switch between logic and emotion. They can blend knowledge, technical skill, and the facts of the situation with the empathy and understanding of their feelings and those of others. This level of mastery makes leaders who achieve it naturally in tune and enormously effective at their job. They are able to harness their own full potential and encourage it in others.

How do you know when you have reached this level of self-mastery? You know you have met certain milestones when:

- You are able to accomplish tasks while being mindful of your team's responsibilities and how it may affect them and their jobs.
- You consider all the potential consequences of your actions before you take action.
- You are easily able to delay gratification when other things take precedence, especially when those things are more important to others.
- You are humble and realize your preservation ego is rarely right. (If you think your ego is right, think again.)
- You can say with confidence and humility that if someone were to ask your team, they would honestly and enthusiastically describe you as: disciplined, persistent, loyal, caring, empathetic, and well intentioned.

So, ask yourself today:

1. Which of these areas am I strong in and would others agree with me?
2. Which ones could I improve on?
3. What have others pointed out that I need to work on? (Start with the one that could have the most positive impact on your team.)

Creating self-awareness will allow you to work on blind spots that may be affecting your natural ability to lead and mentor others. These blind spots may create a lack of trust and confidence on the part of your team. By shining a light into these areas and strategically working to improve them, you will only become a stronger leader that your team can learn from, trust, and follow to achieve even greater potential.

> *"Humans are the only creatures in the world that will follow an unstable leader."*
> —**Cesar Milan**

THE COMPOSURE PENDULUM

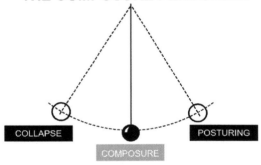

THE COMPOSURE PENDULUM:

COLLAPSE · COMPOSURE · POSTURING

Designed by Chase Hughes, Applied Behavioral Research

To level up your self-mastery abilities, you need to be able to measure if you are improving, staying the same, or going backwards. You need to be sure that what you measure improves. This is where the composure pendulum comes in. As we move from working internally to getting a better understanding of how to control the dials and intensity of our emotions, we need to have the ability to measure our actions in a scientific and non-emotional manner. This, like any skill, is how we fine-tune our actions and create the kind of muscle memory that becomes second nature. It is here that I personally have experienced and have seen my clients take the greatest leaps forward. Through this process, many say they have seen the most noticeable changes in their leader.

Chase Hughes, my mentor and a twenty plus year navy veteran who single-handedly revamped the CIA's intelligence community and the FBI's influence, communication, behavior, and interrogation operating procedures, is a best-selling author, whose book "Phrase Seven" is being made into a Netflix series. Chase is considered the number one expert in his field, and he created the composure pendulum.

www. chasehughes.com

As a behavioral scientist, Chase is always looking for data points to determine accuracy in duplication of any method. He designed the composure method in order to level up the intelligence agents so they could apply the methodologies more effectively. This model was able to help him, and his students measure how the external factors of their environment affected their ability to maintain composure and why.

MEASURING COMPOSURE

noun: **composure**

1. the state or feeling of being calm and in control of oneself.

While we are already working internally (self-mastery), the composure pendulum helps track the success of the execution of that work in your day-to-day life. If you are left or right of the top of that triangle, then you are not in composure. Depending on the situation, your reaction is to either posture or collapse. If you're one millimeter to the right, then you're in the zone of posture, or if you're a millimeter to the left, you're in the zone collapse. What do we mean by that? There are a lot of ways that we can posture or collapse. And we see this in people that we deal with and people that we talk to all the time. It can be seen in ourselves as well.

Posture. We see people that over posture themselves when they feel a little bit threatened. Like a rattlesnake shaking its rattle, these people are making sure everyone knows that they mean business. They are all bark and no bite. And that tends to be their behavioral pattern instead of composure.

Collapse. From a verbal perspective, we see people that collapse when they speak to others. They become afraid of conflict, so they back down without a fight. They give up when things seem too hard.

All of us have done both of these many times throughout our lives. But this is our first data point. At the end of the day, you are tracking yourself to determine what triggers move you from composure. We can observe this in others and how they handle both emotional triggers and self-mastery.

Let's use a financial example. You may have experienced this, seen this, or done this yourself. A new entrepreneur or salesperson is prone to collapse. When they are in a situation where they need to discuss money, for example, closing or setting a price, they are not confident in themselves and are afraid of rejection. They might say something like this.

"I'd like to come out there and provide you with our consultation solution. My rates are $9,000 a day."

The customer on the other phone says, "I'm not sure that's in our budget."

The sales entrepreneur responds with, "I mean that's just our starting point. I haven't heard your budget yet. We could probably give you guys a really good deal. I can actually give you like forty percent off, not a big deal."

The client on the other end still doesn't say anything.

So, our new entrepreneur who is now in full collapse free fall says, "Well, you know, I mean we could probably back down. I could just do it for like seventy-five percent off, and you know we can give you a couple of bonuses and give you a bunch of free stuff. I can even come down to you guys for a month."

The client stays silent which prompts our collapsing business owner or sales rep to say in a jittery voice, "You know what, I'll write you a check. I'll pay you, and I'll come down there and do consulting."

I know this is an overly exaggerated example, however, the pressure of the situation and the lack of self-awareness creates a focus on the fact that to that person it is more important to get a "yes" and save face than it is to maintain composure and walk away. We hear people like this in conversations all the time, especially new leaders that feel they must prove themselves, know everything, have all the answers, and be the most important person in the room.

We see posturing from guys like Dan Lok who is best known for being the founder and chairman of Closers.com, the world's #1 virtual closer network. These guru types who want to force their hourly wage rate down other people's throat and say, "This is how much I'm worth. I'm not taking a penny less or I'm not going to work with you. I don't care if you're a charitable organization. I don't care if you save kids from poverty, I'm not going to give you any kind of discount."

We can see all that comes from people who posture and from those that collapse. The good thing is that all of this is correctable. We can adjust and change the areas that move us to each side of the pendulum if we become more aware of what we are doing and why. To do this effectively, we must first identify the inertia that creates that movement in the pendulum. And that starts with conscious and non-emotional tracking of when it happens.

All we're doing is tracking; however, it is important to note that the tracking is not about perfectionism, or self-abuse. That would sabotage your progress. All you are doing is watching the data. This will give you the ability to wrap your hand around the steering wheel and start taking control. It's the awareness that we're generating from day-to-day. We don't need some kind of a long, drawn-out plan with special milestones and different colored highlighters, sticky notes, and a bunch of notebooks. We just need to keep a watchful eye on certain things, environments, situations, people, and pressures we have identified as triggers.

HOW TO USE YOUR TRACKED DATA

I have trained hundreds of people, and the number one thing that I've noticed is that when a person fails in their leadership, communication, and self-mastery journey, the failure can almost always be traced back to them collapsing or posturing instead of maintaining composure.

I can talk to a person and in a short period of time I can determine whether they're a collapse person, posturing person, or, for the most part, a composed person. Nobody stays in composure all the time. A natural way to determine a composer is how we act when the unexpected happens, for example, being stung by a wasp. If you've ever been stung by a wasp, how you reacted tells you where you went on the pendulum.

I have seen a salt of the earth farmer, stung by a wasp. Before it buried its butt into his neck, he simply said "mm," and pulled it out, tossing it back into the air so it could fly on. Most people would scream, smash it, even stomp on it with 6,000 times the amount of force necessary to kill it. Most of us would have postured against it. People can collapse or posture in any situation, it doesn't matter whether it is talking to a cashier, in the waiting room at the dentist, driving in traffic, or even standing in a crowded elevator.

So how do we start to capture this data?

Start with a 3x5" card or in the "Notes" app on your cell phone. Here is what I use to track. Feel free to make it your own.

Number of days in a month

What you are scoring	Trait	1	2	3	4	5	6	7	8	9	10	11	12	13	14	15	16	17	18	19	20	21	22	23	24	25	26	27	28	29	30	31

Monthly Development Tracking

Trait		
Pendulum		
Confidence		
Discipline		
Leadership		
Gratitude		
Enjoyment		

At the end of each day, rank each section daily from 1 (lowest) to 5 (highest)
For **PENDULUM** use C for collapse, P for posture, and CP for composure instead of numbers

Notes / self-observation / wins or comparison to last month's goals

Goals for next month

At the end of every day, take a moment to reflect on different situations where you recognized that you lost control of the emotional steering wheel. What was the moment when you recognized you moved from composure to posture? Write down in your notes:

- The environment (office, work, home, board meeting, client's office, etc...)
- The situations (one-on-one meeting, presenting to the team, or meeting with my boss)
- The moment you realized you moved the pendulum (being challenged, boss asked me a question I did not have the answer to, or had to have a difficult conversation with a teammate)

Score yourself in that moment using the traits above.

(PENDULUM: C, P, or CP Traits: confidence 1-5, discipline 1-5, leadership 1-5, gratitude 1-5)

Review the day as a whole and score yourself overall. This and the notes will start to present a clearer picture of what your triggers are, how you handle them, and going back to self-mastery, what you need to dial up or dial down to achieve a more favorable circumstance.

This all sounds like a lot of work, and it is. To be an exceptional leader, you must possess a student's mindset. You will find you are always learning, adjusting, and fine-tuning all of these things. Great leaders have a natural curiosity about themselves and the world around them. I believe it is because they know if they can present their very best version of themselves, they just might help, inspire, or even guide others to their best selves. They are constantly seeking to find the flaws and the solutions to improve themselves.

SCAN ME :PDF
Pendulum Development Tracker

THE IMPORTANCE OF SOCIAL SUPPORT

As a new leader, the greatest challenge you may face is the balance between working on yourself and being able to make the decisions required by your role. One of the greatest mistakes I see new leaders make is assuming they must carry this burden alone. The first sign I observe that tells me new leaders are doing this is their lack of communication with their team. They bottle it in, they struggle internally, and think they need to have the answers to earn the trust of their team (or beat them into submission by yelling and being angry).

What I admire about the next generation of leaders that are rising to their new roles is that they take a collaborative approach to solving problems. They naturally have a desire to build teamwork, increase communication and trust, and have a greater purpose that they can communicate to the team. These are all fundamental aspirations that would make any team successful. Trouble starts when they realize not everyone on the team has the same level of desire in those areas as they do.

As well intentioned as the next generation leader you are, you may not have any control over the hiring or the makeup of the team you are asked to lead. This blindsides some leaders and even paralyzes them. The driving force, motivation, and measurement of success for that leader are their people. If that same team is not as enthusiastic as the leader wants them to be, it can be a hard pill to swallow. It has been my experience that in most cases the team is supportive in those ideas and leadership style. The key is for the leader to know how to express those ideas in such a way that it aligns with the values and reason each individual team member has for being there.

This is not always as simple as it sounds, especially if you have multiple generations on your team. Each culture has a set of expectations that govern how they want you to lead and deliver results. You were once part of the team, and now you are in charge. Or my favorite, you were brought into an established team because their beloved leader was fired. That is every new leader's nightmare.

Regardless of the situation you find yourself in, there is one skill that will help you connect, influence, and begin to earn their trust: effective communication. You might say, "I am a good communicator," and by all intents and purposes, you may be. Under these circumstances, it requires an understanding of science, behavior, and human nature to make your efforts that much more successful. As you will find in the coming chapters, the more you know and understand about your team and what makes each one of them tick, the more effective you will be at inspiring them, leading them, and helping them achieve their goals.

CHAPTER 3:

"YOU ARE A BLEND OF ALL BEHAVIORAL STYLES"

Throughout our human evolution, communication has been the catalyst of change and of choice. If you think about every major change in human history, each was pre-empted by a moving speech. A call to war, the space race, presidential elections, a football coach at half time; each provide an inspirational moment that drives people to act. Words move the soul. As a new leader, this is one skill that when added to the self-mastery training, will elevate your confidence and create a sense of trust with your team. There is a simple formula to help you identify the communication style, pace, and focus of anyone you speak with. This formula will guide you on how to adjust your message so that what you say is not only understood but is said in a way that aligns to each person's values and motivations.

WHAT IF WE ALL CAME WITH AN INSTRUCTIONAL MANUAL?

We all make decisions based on perception. Perception, in turn, is based on our experiences, our up bringing, values, and knowledge of the subject. Your brain works this way and therefore, the same is true of the individuals you lead. The challenge is that no one has all their knowledge, values, and experiences written on their foreheads for you to easily read. Or do they? Once you learn to recognize simple words, pace, tone, and behavior, you will see it is like reading an open book. Once you learn these simple techniques, you will see we all walk around with an instructional manual. The difference is that nobody told you or taught you how to read it, until now.

UNDERSTANDING BEHAVIOR

We must first identify what behavior style we use, so we know how it is being perceived and where we need to adapt so that our listeners understand and feel comfortable with the information. Understanding how to communicate and connect with other people is imperative to any long-term success. When you build relationships, behavior is the key word, not personality, because behaviors never lie but personalities can change based on the environment or what the client may be feeling at the moment. Learn to address the behavior of the moment and you will always create a solid connection.

Understanding human behavior will allow you to clearly see two critical issues necessary to master the dialect of leadership:

1. Your own needs, drivers, and blind spots
2. Your team members' needs, drivers, and perceived value

To skip this fundamental process in the language of strategic communication is to miss the key principle that will allow you to clearly communicate with each team member. This is the piece I have found most leaders need to have success long term. This piece acts like a translator that enables you to hear and understand your employee's common language and to respond quickly and fluently in that language.

Why is this important? As we have discovered, **strategic communication** is based on **perceived** value which, in turn, is based on benefits, results, and solutions. These elements are necessary before your clients are willing to buy or refer any business.

SCAN ME : PODCAST EPISODE
The behaviors intro. What you don't know may be
hurting your virtual perception

THE FOUR LANGUAGES OF LEADERSHIP

Prior to this chapter, we took a wide view of self-mastery performance and the importance of communication. Now we are coming in for a closer view, and a laser-focused discussion of the four different dialects of communication. This will help you learn the universal language of strategic conversations.

As you read the descriptions of the four languages of leadership, you will see they are four different styles. You will identify with some more than others, if not find a bit of your leadership style and identity in all of them. There will be, however, one particular style that you feel the most comfortable with. This is your common language, what makes you "tick." In the following chapters, we will take a closer look at what that "tick" is and why it "ticks."

Every leadership style has strengths that make it successful in some situations. Each one also has blind spots that can create uncomfortable, embarrassing, and even toxic environments. The information you're about to experience will teach you how to recognize these attributes in yourself as well as your team.

There are four different styles of leader that I have identified: the Doer, the Influencer, the Supporter, and the Calculator. Understanding where your own strengths lie within this framework can help you make the most of your personal leadership style.

The Doer is exemplified by Steve Jobs. They are naturally hard working and fast paced. They are results driven, they place a high value on time, and they like to challenge the status quo.

When dealing with a Doer, be brief and to the point. Don't ask rhetorical questions and don't attempt to order them around.

SCAN ME: YouTube Video
The D team member

The Influencer is naturally fun loving and can make friends with anyone. Ellen DeGeneres is a good example of this type of leader. They negotiate conflict, are optimistic, and look for the good in others. When dealing with an Influencer, it is important to stress excitement and look engaged. Don't focus on facts and figures, try to smile and have fun.

SCAN ME: YouTube Video
The I team member

The Supporter wants things to be fair for all involved. Gandhi was a supportive type of leader. They want to approach the team from the bottom up, nurturing the soil so that everyone has an equitable chance to succeed. When talking to a Supporter, it is best to start with a personal comment and slowly work towards your business agenda. Diving right in won't give them time to adjust or make them feel validated.

SCAN ME: YouTube Video
The S team member

The Calculator is naturally focused and logical. Nelson Mandela is an example of this type of leader. They are interested in results and need details, rules, and a bulletproof process. They are conscientious and steady, reliable to a fault. When communicating with a Calculator, make sure your message is organized and direct. Take time to prepare your case in advance.

SCAN ME: YouTube Video
The C team member

	Doer	Influencer	Supporter	Calculator
Examples	Steve Jobs	Ellen DeGeneres	Mahatma Gandhi	Nelson Mandela
Qualities	Hardworking Fast-paced Results-driven Time conscious Challenges the status quo	Fun-loving Extremely friendly Negotiates conflicts Optimistic Good-natured	Fair to all Builder Nurturing Inclusive Humble	Focused Logical Detail-oriented Conscientious Reliable
Warning	No rhetorical questions. They are direct in communication so do not go around the bush when dealing with them.	They don't get excited with numbers and figures. To capture their attention, be excited, look engaged, and smile and have fun.	Take it slow. They need to see your real motives before they trust you. Give them time to get to know you better.	Be prepared. They appreciate when you come with an organized proposal.

All of these methods have their strong points and their weaknesses. None of them are "good" or "bad," just different. There are ineffective leaders that want to lead with an iron fist. They want complete control because in their minds, that is the best way to ensure loyalty. They don't see the effect that kind of fear-based environment has on the employees downstream. Obviously, this isn't my preferred leadership style because when you look at how it affects employees, they aren't happy. They live in fear of losing their jobs, and they question every decision they make.

I've had other leaders who are more concerned with creating a community collaborative. There are downsides to that approach as well. People want direction, they want someone who will be responsible for the product or the process when it is released. A true collaborative can leave employees feeling unanchored.

Really good leaders have a sense of themselves, their emotional quotient, their charisma, and their communication style. They're very clear about where the team is going. That's what attracts more people. They bring a great message, and they also have a clear direction that the team can build upon. Their confidence in who they are exudes confidence to everyone else.

SCAN ME: PDF
What Leader Style Are You?

THE COMFORT ZONE

Your internal desire to have your needs met creates your behavior.

- Your behavior sends messages to your employees.
- Your employees respond individually to all messages you send, verbal and nonverbal

Even if your employees only sense the messages subconsciously and cannot tell you what they pick up from you, their sense of what you are communicating still drives their behaviors. When your behavior communicates that you are not genuine or are working to meet your own needs (lack of self-mastery), you create a sense of caution within your team. When they sense that you are working to meet *their* needs, they will tend to trust you more and feel a closer connection (at least in a business sense). The resulting trust and connection will lead to better performance.

Every behavioral style has different natural tendencies. These tendencies act as "comfort zones"—the areas where people feel most comfortable. By understanding your employees' behavioral language, you will be able to create a "comfort zone" and adjust your behavior accordingly to connect and communicate more effectively. This will create the kind of relationship that makes your client comfortable to do business with you and become an advocate and a repeat customer.

Have you ever been to a foreign country where you did not speak the language and did not know the customs? How was that experience for you? For most people, it was a bit scary, frustrating, and maybe uncomfortable. Life is difficult when you are not able to communicate or navigate the basics of everyday life including transportation, food, and directions. Think of each behavioral style as its own country that speaks a very specific language. They each have different customs and when two people with the same styles interact, their common language creates an instant sense of belonging.

Let's unpack the language and needs for each leadership style:

SCAN ME: PODCAST SERIES
Learn about how to connect with
each behavior style simply and confidently

Each style has different perceptions. My colleagues and I brought together one hundred high-performing salespeople and presented them with a series of facts. During our research, we discovered that their reactions were based on their behavioral language.

The **DOMINANT** employees wanted to know, *"What is going on here?"*

The **INTERACTIVE** employees inquired, *"Who is invited to this function?"*

The **STEADY** employees wondered, *"How do we need to do this project?"*

The **CALCULATING** employees asked, *"Why are we doing this?"*

The specifics of the facts did not determine the value to the conversation. The **perception** of each style and what they heard and how they interpreted the information was eye-opening. By understanding the behavioral language of your employees, you can increase the perceived value of your message as well as helping them to communicate effectively with you.

> *"All our knowledge has its origins in our perceptions."*
> **—Leonardo Davinci**

Sadly, very few leaders focus on behavioral styles and what they mean for communication. This is why, when you apply and learn the four languages of leadership, you will have shortened your leadership learning curve tremendously. If you can learn to identify and communicate in the common language of your team, your leadership skills will accelerate to the speed of life.

THE BREAKDOWN

Each style is important in its own unique way. Together they balance each other and when they all work in harmony, there is nothing that can keep you from success. As you read through each description, think about your team: employees, clients, and even family members. See if you can determine which region they would relate to the most. Which style do you associate with more than fifty percent of the time? This will help you begin to identify different employees' languages and how they may differ from yours, allowing you to appreciate and comprehend their unique perceptions. This will also provide you with a game plan to create that comfort zone that will foster effective conversations and lead to productive outcomes.

The only way to perfect a language is through practice. But before we can look at each employee's individual communication style, it is important to see and recognize them in the real world. Understanding perception is the key to connection. To identify what behavioral style the person you are speaking with is using, begin simply by observing and listening to that person's pace and priorities.

> *"If a man does not keep pace with his companions, perhaps it is because he hears a different drummer. Let him step to the music which he hears, however measured or far away."*
> **—Henry David Thoreau**

PACE

Pace is that internal rhythm we all tend to live by, the speed at which we are most comfortable. Some live for speed, others need the security of doing things slowly. It is where we feel at home or where we retreat to when we feel scared or cornered. Pace is the starting point of your connection to your employees. Though the value of the discussion has not been decided, the decision to move forward with your conversation may rely heavily on pace. This is where you can begin to create the comfort zone for your individual employees to decide whether they will listen and focus on what you have to say. The following will provide you with the directions necessary to begin to see and connect with any client's pace.

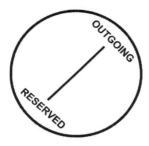

On the top half of the style map is the **outgoing** or fast-paced employee. Just as the name suggests, these team members are fast-paced, autobahn style—slam the accelerator and apologize for it later. This area is energetic. Team members who are comfortable here are driven, they decide fast and think fast and tend to be loud. They can be described as:

- Optimistic
- Energetic
- Involved
- Decisive
- Enthusiastic
- Always on the move

They live by the word "go." New York City and Las Vegas come to mind when I think of this group.

On the lower half of the style map is the complete opposite, the **reserved** or slow-paced area. You can float and relax here, as if you were on a slow winding river. This group is not in a hurry; team members take their time to do everything. Their movements, thoughts, and decisions are not rushed but thought out carefully and with precision. They are a cautious group and reluctant to get involved in too many activities. The employees of the lower half of the map can be described as:

- Cautious
- Concerned
- Reluctant
- Contemplative
- Discerning

They live by the "measure twice and cut once" philosophy. Small Montana towns and the Bayous of New Orleans come to mind when I think of this group.

It is here that I find most new leaders struggle. When we are under stress, pressure, or fatigue, we will go at the pace we are most comfortable with. We don't even know we are doing it. So, if you are naturally fast paced and you are holding your first meeting with seasoned team members, you may not realize you are speaking a bit faster than you would normally. If some of your team members are more reserved, they may just tune you out.

When a leader attempts to go in the opposite direction and pretend to be something they are not, the results are disastrous. A person who is naturally fast and trying to be slow for too long will come across as condescending and disingenuous. When there is a disconnect between who you genuinely are and what you are presenting, your non-verbal language tells the person who is listening that something is not right. It is a gut feeling that creates a warning.

There is a difference between adapting and pretending. Adapting is taking the time to learn some of the key phrases and customs of that foreign country you are going to visit. Pretending is trying to use high school Spanish you learned thirty years ago and thinking you are fluent.

Application:

List two names of clients that have recently purchased from you, and determine what pace they were:

Name:_____(Pace) Fast or Slow

Name:_____(Pace) Fast or Slow

Based on what you have just learned, what would you do differently to connect with each client?

PRIORITY

Priority is the second dichotomy that determines how well you communicate with your employees. If the pace of your conversation allows you to connect, then *priority* will help you to increase the value of your words.

Priorities are the reason **why** employees of each style buy in to ideas, suggestions, and training. These priorities are the primary fuel that drives each team member to follow you, give 110 percent, or come to work every day with a great attitude. The priority part of the map has two sides, the **task** side and the **people** side. They are both equally important yet approach the same situation from different perspectives.

Task-oriented employees (left side) like to do things, make plans, or work on projects. They strive to have a well-oiled, fine-tuned working machine, whether through their own process or the client experience of their workflow. They are always striving for perfection. They are extremely competitive and will find a way to win. They are also considered "high tech." They like to have the newest technology and gadget on the market, sometimes for show, but mostly because it helps them get the task done better.

They create checklists and focus on tasks. Just like soldiers, they must accomplish the mission at all costs. Their priorities tend to be on accomplishing a project, assignment, or job. Some words that define the left side of the style map are:

- Process
- Organization
- Function
- Program
- Plan
- Project

Who comes to mind on your team when you read these words? Can you think of an employee like this, who is focused on results and accuracy? They define value by the number of tasks completed or by the results. Why? Because the outcome of their work is a direct reflection of who they are. They will evaluate their achievement or contribution by one of those two mediums.

As a leader you must align your conversations and questions to those two elements: results and accuracy. Task-oriented team members do not tend to enjoy small talk. They are professional and focus on work first.

People-orientated employees (right side) enjoy fun and being hospitable to others. This is *not* to say that the task-oriented folks are inhospitable or do not have fun, not at all. The difference is that the people-oriented workers make it a priority and the task-oriented folks focus on the task they need to accomplish. The people side of the nation loves having conversations, getting to know one another and look for social support; those employees are just wired that way. Their priorities tend to be more about relationships, people, and, above all, **fun**! These are the team members you ask to set up the company party.

Some words that define this group are:

- Feelings
- Relationships
- Caring
- Sharing
- Emotions
- Friendships

As a leader you must understand what motivates and drives each member of your team. If you have people-oriented team members, they need socialization to feel a connection. Each orientation is like a battery: if it is plugged in the right place, they will be energized and ready to go. If you put these employees in the wrong place, in a negative social situation, their batteries will be drained, and their performance and attitude will be poor. These small areas of understanding can mean the difference between a high-performing team with great morale and a destructive one with a revolving door. Consider which of your employees might be people-oriented and who might be more task-oriented.

- People-oriented employees focus on experiences rather than fact.
- Task-oriented employees make decisions based on facts and logic.

THE FOUR REGIONS

When you put pace and priority together, you can easily use this to discover anyone's style on the map.

Now that you have all of the four regions together, here is the secret to making it all work following the OLA method. OLA stands for *Observe, Listen, Adapt.* You can observe and listen for each of the four indicators (fast or slow pace, task or people priority) to determine which behavioral language your team members are speaking. Here's how it works:

1. **OBSERVE** mannerisms—Fast-paced or outgoing employees talk using their hands frequently. Slow-

paced or reserved employees may exhibit soft body movements.

2. **LISTEN** for pace. This will be evident during your first conversation. Listen for **task** or **people** words. Task-oriented people will say, "I think." People-oriented employees will say, "I feel." Also listen to the pace they are speaking. Is it FAST or more RESERVED? This should be the first place you adapt your normal pace to match.

3. **ADAPT** your natural style. What have you heard and observed? You will either be slowing down or picking up your pace. Then adjust the focus of the conversation to highlight either the task or the relationships as you determined in the listening phase.

Remember, **pace** creates the comfort zone for connection; priority gives value to the conversation.

The OLA method will help you identify and connect with any person quickly. Start by asking some questions and focusing on the pace and words they are using to adapt your natural style by speaking the language that makes the person you are communicating with more comfortable and focused on what you have to say in the way you intended it.

CHAPTER 4:

DOMINANT, INTERACTIVE, CALCULATING AND STEADY

IDENTIFYING THE FOUR BEHAVIORAL STYLES

Now that you have mastered the OLA, let me show you how to use the same skill to identify the four behavioral styles. As a leader, being able to adjust quickly to the different behaviors and communication needs of your team is critical to your success. If you are applying the self-mastery techniques I spoke of earlier, you will also recognize that ego has no room here. You work for your team; they do not work for you regardless of your title. I can prove it.

If everyone on your team walked out right now, who would that affect the most? I am willing to bet your boss would still want answers from you. On the other hand, if you were fired, would it really disrupt the team's work? Or would you be replaced?

Too often I encounter people that are driven by their title. They are self-focused. Great leaders are team focused. This leads to the ability to effectively identify the behaviors and preferred conversation style of each of their team members. When this skill is mastered, you will be able to make every team member feel like they are the most important person in the room.

To identify which of the four styles of leadership someone is using, first we use the same observation techniques of pace and priority.

Pace

- Fast pace and task oriented = Dominant behavioral style
- Fast pace and people oriented = Interactive behavioral style

- Reserved and task oriented = Calculating behavioral style
- Reserved and people oriented = Steady behavioral style

- Fast-paced behaviors = Dominant and Interactive
- Reserved behaviors = Calculating and Steady

Priority

- Task-oriented behavior style = Dominant and Calculating
- People-oriented behavioral styles = Interactive and Steady

The following are a set of quick reference charts that will allow you to determine a person's behavioral style at a glance and give you tips to communicate effectively.

THE DOMINANT STYLE

SCAN ME: AUDIO
Hear more about the
Dominant Style

Overview	Outgoing-Task
Percentage of population	Ten percent
Describing words	Dominant, direct, demanding, decisive, doer
Symbol	The bull -- strength and power
Reason they buy	To accomplish a task or project
Pace	Upbeat, fast intense
Fuel	Results
Need from you	Choice, bottom line, answer, control, do what you say you are going to do.
Comfort zone	Fast, bottom line, getting things done, they buy -- they get in and they get out.
Their mantra	"Be quick, be bright, be gone."

Some examples are Clint Eastwood (as a cowboy or Dirty Harry), John Wayne, Queen Elizabeth, General Patton, Judge Judy, Bobby Knight, and Tiger Woods.

Dominant style employees can complete amazing amounts of work and be critical of poorly performed tasks. They also believe that approval and encouragement can lead to complacency. Due to their direct nature, they might unintentionally intimidate others. You will find that every region has a fuel or a defining need that makes those clients tick as well as a blind spot that creates their biggest challenge. They need only one thing to accomplish their tasks and to get up in the morning. It defines the air they breathe and their reason for living: **RESULTS!**

The DOMINANT employee wants you to be:

- Quick
- To the point
- Confident
- Specific
- Respectful
- Results driven
- Able to provide solutions to their needs

Who are the **dominant** employees on your team?

THE INTERACTIVE STYLE

SCAN ME: AUDIO

Hear more about the
Interactive Style

Overview	Outgoing-People
Percentage of population	Twenty-five to thirty percent
Describing words	Inspiring, interactive, involved, impressive
Symbol	Fireworks---they light up the room and need to be the center of attention.
Reason they buy	Images and popularity
Pace	Fast and popularity
Fuel	Fun
Need from you	Public recognition, smile, to be liked.
Comfort zone	Fun, exciting, prestige, friendly. Interactive people want to know "who?" Who else is wearing it or using it?
Their mantra	*"If you obey all the rules, you miss all the fun."*

Some examples are Howie Mandell, Robin Williams, Jay Leno, Oprah, Kevin Heart, and Lucille Ball.

Whether it is one person or a large crowd, this type thrives on contact with people. They tend to be the WOO-HOO people in the crowd. Gaining everyone's acceptance, love, and admiration gives this type of energy.

Interactive style employees tend be loud, happy, and optimistic. They have the knack of getting close in a very short period of time and can make you feel like you have been friends forever. They are quick with a bright smile that illuminates the room. They can always share a funny story to help you forget your worries. The most important quality you can ever offer an interactive type is **RECOGNITION**. Give them praise and they will love you forever.

Leaders, if you want to connect and communicate effectively with your interactive employee:

- **Smile**. Deep down most INTERACTIVE team members just want to be liked, and a smile shows them that you like them.
- **Laughing** and being personal will set them at ease.
- Making them feel special will also go a long way with this employee.
- Compliment them; they like to **feel that they are the center of attention**.
- Treat them as VIPs and friends. By making them feel like the only person in the crowd, you will show them that they are an important member of the team.

Don't misunderstand these employees. They may love the spotlight and being the center of attention, but this does not necessarily make them snobs or too good for the masses. Yes, there are some like that, however, interactive employees tend to be the most appreciative and genuine towards people who treat them nicely. They are the first to unselfishly share with others without expecting anything in return. Remember, this is their comfort zone, language, and customs and their natural tendency. The more fun and special the environment, the higher the perceived value you are creating for these employees to thrive.

Who are the **interactive** employees on your team?

THE STEADY STYLE

SCAN ME: AUDIO
Hear more about the
Supportive Style

Overview	Reserved-People
Percentage of population	Twenty to thirty-five percent
Describing words	Steady, Stable, Sweet, status quo
Symbol	The scale--represents balance. Steady people are always in the middle as they do not want to hurt anyone's feelings. They want everyone to get along.
Reason they buy	Relationships, familiarity with the product. A feeling of comfort and security.
Pace	Slow
Fuel	Supporting others. peace, and balance
Need from you	A sense of security, familiarity, and appreciation.
Comfort zone	Patience, consistency, predictability, no conflict, relational, and familiar.
Their mantra	*"Can't we all just get along?"*

Some examples are Dr. Martin Luther King Jr., Gandhi, Mother Teresa, Mr. Rogers, and the Dalai Lama.

Words that describe a steady employee:

- Supportive
- Stable
- Cautious
- Kind

My biggest success came from understanding my blind spot and learning how to adjust to it. I learned to speak the **steady** language when it was necessary to build relationships. My greatest accomplishment came with my daughter. As I mentioned before, we are all a blend of all regions. Her predominant behaviors were in the steady and interactive, with a lower dominant (which translates into a very strong-willed drama queen). She was sensitive about her feelings and protective of others, never hesitating to express how she felt. For ten years, we fought over everything. It seemed we could never do anything that did not end in a fight.

At 14 years old, my daughter was having trouble identifying her feelings, so she would lash out. I was fortunate enough to learn human behavior and soon realized what I was unknowingly doing to create this war zone. I realized my voice, deep and forceful, sounded as if I was yelling at her, even when I was speaking in a normal tone. Talking to her face-to-face made her feel uncomfortable and combative. So, I adjusted. I spoke more slowly and lowered my voice. I listened and waited. I sat next to her with my arm around her and asked questions. In 48 hours, I repaired ten years of war. She is now 21, in college, and we speak every day. I have taught her to cook and even been a shoulder for her to cry on. By simply speaking her language and seeing her perspective, I now have a great relationship with my daughter.

Steady style employees like a calm, easygoing environment where there is a predictable routine and things remain pretty much the same. They thrive in an environment where bonding with individuals is possible. They are the peacekeepers; they will often do anything to keep the peace with little or no regard to how it may affect them. They are always behind the scenes to ensure everything runs smoothly and, most importantly, that everyone's needs are met. They may feel like they are imposing and monopolizing your time. Reassure them and show them appreciation. Go out of your way to earn their trust. This will pay dividends; they will be the most loyal clients you will ever have. If you do not take advantage of them or treat them rudely, they will make sure to tell everyone they know about you. Their friends will listen since they know **steady** types do not make decisions lightly.

A Steady employee reacts best to leaders who are:

- Kind
- Pleasant
- Caring
- Patient
- Understanding
- Gentle

Who are the **steady** employees on your team?

THE CALCULATING STYLE

SCAN ME: AUDIO
Hear more about the
Calculating Style

Overview	Reserved-Task
Percentage of population	Twenty to twenty-five percent
Describing words	Cautious, competent, careful, conscientious
Symbol	The magnifying glass. They like to investigate and research everything.
Reason they buy	Quality products or services to assist them in accomplishing their project.
Pace	Slow and precise
Fuel	Quality answers, process, and procedure
Need from you	Ability to research independently, excellence, and value. Individual focus and attention. Knowledgeable staff.
Comfort zone	Structure, accuracy, details, and correctness. Logical and simple online research and buying procedures.
Their mantra	*"The cautious seldom err."* ~Confucius

Some examples are: Sergeant Friday, Einstein, Sir Isaac Newton, Mr. Spock, Steve Jobs, Sherlock Holmes, Leonardo Davinci, Benjamin Franklin, and Bill Gates.

Calculating style employees carefully explore all options and study all related information. These team members will validate the quality of information and develop procedures, which will prevent mistakes. They love graphs and analyzing facts. Their cognitive skills allow them to think of ways to improve an idea. They will go to any length to achieve excellence.

This region is very thorough in everything they do, which is why **calculating** type employees ask a lot of questions. They will have done countless hours of research and comparison before deciding what to buy. The word perfectionist can best describe them. Think of Sherlock Holmes and his powers of deduction, which were always based on research and facts. "Elementary, my dear Watson, elementary."

Words that describe the calculating employee:

- Cautious
- Competent
- Careful
- Conscientious

Calculating types tend to be extremely analytical. They plan the work and work the plan. These team members will most likely know more about your product or service than you do. If they did not initiate the sales process, they will not buy immediately. They will gather information and research it later, double-checking for accuracy. These clients require trust through fact verification before they can build a relationship and rapport. Their comfort zone comes from accurate information, quality answers, and a process or procedure they can follow.

Calculating employees, in particular, would rather focus on data and communicate via technology, as they are not fond of human interaction. That does not make them bad people. It is simply how they are wired and what makes them tick. When leading this style of behavior:

- Provide accurate and relevant information. Let them direct the conversation. Your focus should be on the logical and accurate delivery of information.
- Set up an appointment to speak with them, they do not appreciate drop ins. Don't be late.
- Have your thoughts and ideas in order and make sure they lead to a logical conclusion.
- Send any information ahead of time so they have time to review, research, and be prepared.
- Stick with the facts; no small talk. They have an agenda they need to accomplish.
- Remember this employee thrives on efficiency. They are great at looking at a problem and breaking down what went wrong and what it would take to fix it.

The Calculating employee responds better to leaders who are:

- Accommodating
- Accurate
- Reasonable
- Accountable
- Knowledgeable of the product or service you are selling
- Honest
- Sincere
- Structured
- To the point

These employees are often mistaken for cold and uncaring, but that is far from the truth. They are simply operating from the logical point of view which, in most cases, is void of emotion. Just as all the other employees on the style map, they have a unique common language: logic, process, and procedure. They are the agents of organization and rules. It is because of their attention to details that more often than not, they pick up on those small areas that keep us out of jail and ensure that the quality of the product is always above and beyond expectations.

Who do you have on your team who is a **calculating** employee?

CHAPTER 5:

GROWTH IS THE GOAL

VALUES

One of the basic themes that keeps resurfacing in my work is values. As a leader, you need to align your team's values with the values of the organization. If there is a disconnect, it will affect the team's ability to perform. If the organization itself doesn't live up to its values, you might have to bring it up in an executive meeting, and it might not be easy. But without a clear understanding of values, any work will be meaningless. I have a quick and easy assessment that you can share with your team to determine whether you are all on the same page with your values. I embarrassed a CFO one time. He wanted to introduce a new sales system, but he was failing at it completely. The customers were just not responding, and sales were declining rather than improving.

SCAN ME : GIFT
Your Free Behavior Assessment

I said, "So let me understand something, because I'm confused. You just spent half a million dollars in sales training, because you wanted a more relational approach to your customers to build more trust and value."

"Right," he said.

"But you failed to build that trust and value in your own team." He was driving his employees through fear, tying their sales figures to their job security. "That's being a hypocrite. How can you have your team do something that you yourself are not doing? If you can't sell this to your team, how can you hold them accountable to sell it to their clients?"

If he wanted a relational approach with his clients but was using a fear-based transactional approach with his employees, no wonder it wasn't working. There was a value disconnect. On one hand, he was stressing the value of trust and relationships, but on the other hand, he was promoting mistrust and paranoia in his staff. It doesn't have to be this stark for employees to notice when a company doesn't live up to its own values. It is one of the chief reasons people become disenchanted with their employer. That hypocrisy makes it difficult to summon the energy to perform.

It can be hard, when you are invested in the corporate culture, to be that blunt with your CFO. One of the benefits that I offer as an independent consultant is a fresh perspective. I can have those difficult conversations that no one else in your organization can have. I can see the way people are interacting and go straight to the source.

Malcom Gladwell reported that once a company hits fifty employees, it becomes all about silos. That's a visual way of explaining what happens when an individual or a team functions separately from other teams and individuals. There is no interaction between departments. They are islands within the larger sea, or silos of grain on a farm. If you can keep a company between forty and forty-five employees, it still has that family feel. Titles are irrelevant and people are more willing to work for each other, regardless of the task. No matter how many locations they have, the moment a company crosses that threshold of forty-five, employees start looking at their work as a "job" versus a team or a family. There is a culture shift that is created because more employees require more supervision. Responsibilities become more focused and there is less conversation around the water cooler.

Larger organizations can address this development by keeping departments under forty-five people. Working teams can be even smaller. When you deliberately maintain groups of employees at the ideal level, even a global corporation can feel like a family business.

As a new leader, you need to be intentional about the culture you create. Realize that you need to work within the confines of your current organization, and that the size of that organization plays a big part. Choose people to work together not just because they're similar, but because they fit into the specific culture, whether it's an innovative culture, a family culture, or a hardcore alpha culture. You have to know if they are adding value to it because you need your team to work well together. As a leader, you define the mission, the structure, and the process, and by putting the right people in place and being true to your values, you can get the most out of your staff.

REMOVING GROWTH ANXIETY

Uncertainty creates anxiety. The brain is looking for information to navigate the world; it is a predicting machine. The more information we get, the more comfortable we are because we can predict outcomes based on past experiences that are similar. This is different from fear. With fear, you can point to the cause of the fear—snake, robber, heights, bugs. With anxiety, you cannot put a finger on the cause of why you are feeling anxious. You can tell the difference between fear and anxiety by simply focusing on the conversation you are having internally. If most of the conversation is about asking what if, you are anxious and seeking information; your body is naturally attempting to determine danger or safety, so it goes over every possible situation looking for a match so it can determine the best course of action. Fear, on the other hand, makes you go either running, frozen, or fighting. There is no guessing or conversation going on in your head except for some self-talk to overcome the fear (positive choice of words that are appropriate at the moment). Lack of information creates stress and uncertainty because the brain is unable to plan for the future. We all saw this in the first few months of the pandemic, when businesses closed, and masks were first discouraged and then mandated. Everyone was operating on what small amount of information they could squeeze from scientists and elected officials. Stress levels rose and anxiety went through the roof.

There doesn't have to be a global emergency to create a cloud of uncertainty. The market's ups and downs are enough to worry investors. Business leaders are focused on making payroll, on generating new market share, and increasing profits. A credit card processing company, Gravity Payments, solved the issue of employee anxiety in an innovative way. The CEO raised everyone's minimum salary to $70,000 because they found that at $70 to $75,000, most people's anxiety went away. They were no longer worried about the mortgage or car payments, and they could focus completely on the task at hand.

The CEO had the crazy idea that, "If we eliminate our employees' anxiety around making enough money we can grow the business." So, he cut his own salary, and gave everyone raises. He discovered that most people stop feeling like they are in survival mode when they are making a minimum of $75,000. He made every single employee autonomous with ownership of their own ideas and the ability to contribute to growth. In an interview with one of his employees, a sales rep was documenting his own growth. He came up with a great idea to improve the customer experience. He went to his manager and the manager said, "Here's how it works. You work out the process, the plan, the cost, how you're going to measure it, and then you come back and present it to us. If we like it, you're in charge of executing."

Just because something is uncertain, doesn't necessarily mean it's unsafe. If you look at your mind, your upbringing, your experiences, your failures, and your successes, all of these create filters that you unconsciously apply to anything new. When you find yourself in an uncertain situation, your mind brings up the filters and runs through them. You match the unknown against what you have experienced in the past. And that determines how you see the world. But the thing is, it's subconscious; we don't even realize this is happening. Our brains tell us, "This situation looks a lot like that time we messed up and got hurt, so let's be cautious, or let's avoid this altogether." It's a system designed to help us survive, but it leads to a lot of unnecessary anxiety. How often have you thought something was going to be worse than what it really was? More often than not, our brains tell us that new things are going to be worse than they turn out to be. Anxiety serves a purpose, but it can also block us from learning and growing.

Money is one obstacle to high performance which can serve as an incentive. Trust and autonomy are other motivators that are used less often but are sometimes more effective than a simple pay raise. In an uncertain environment, people get anxious. They tend to freeze up and the creative process stagnates. As a leader, your job is to provide your team with as much information as you can. Wherever possible, remove barriers to self-sufficiency and allow your employees to trust in you. Even in uncertain economic times, having a competent leader who does not hide critical information will go a long way toward easing anxiety and increasing productivity.

LETTING GO

Over time, several organizations become comfortable with the devil they know. Change seems more challenging to make than just putting up with what they have. This is especially true when just doing what you are doing still pays the bills. This mindset is best illustrated with a client we worked with who owned a specialized IT consulting company. They are adept in analyzing and implementing a system that could handle many systems and support. Edward, the owner, had a partner named Thomas with whom he had started the company. Edward wanted to grow, and the demand was there, yet no matter what he did, they seemed to lack the manpower to handle the projects they had. To fulfill their clients' expectations, they needed specialists in different aspects of technology from code writing, hardware, systems, and more. No matter how many people he would bring in, they did not stay long enough to grow. When he reached out to me, he explained that the company would hire enough people to grow, but they would quit soon after that. After a seven-stage business analysis, we discovered two things:

- He never shed the chaos of the start-up phase, and;
- His partner was dragging the business down.

He had been with his business partner for ten years, but based on our assessment, the toxic elements all point to Thomas. There were all kinds of responsibilities, communication, data management, and expected results not being delivered, all of which affected the bottom line and, worst, the team in general. We identified through exit interviews that the main reason Edward's newer employees were quiting was due to Thomas and largely in the way he spoke to them. According to them, he treated them as just tools and numbers, and he's demanding and barking orders without respect for them as a person. It took him six months, but he finally fired his partner and went back to the beginning to build his team fresh. He created a new business model, identified his target audience, and restructured the company so that it would run more efficiently.

Now he's up to twenty-one employees. If you walk into his office, you'll see a whiteboard on the wall that says, "What do I need to do? What does my team need to do?" They've gone from almost being bankrupt to generating over three million dollars per year in profits. They have a very comfortable growth pattern; they just had the wrong employees.

One of the biggest challenges any leader faces is getting the right people into the right positions. Edward is an IT professional. He wasn't a salesperson and he struggled with customer relations. He was not comfortable in doing those things so he deffered to his partner to take charge, and had a blind eye to the fall out because the revenue was still coming in. In the beginning, he had all these techies who were also supposed to do customer service. They didn't have the right training; they didn't know how to communicate and were not aware of the mission, vision, or values with which they could align their personal values and on-the-job objectives. More importantly, there wasn't a process for them to utilize their strengths and provide the quality of service the customers expected.

Once we identified that at a company retreat, they started to innovate. They implemented a vision , mission and standards as well as a ticket system to streamline the customer communications. The system helped them to keep track of work orders and get to every issue in a timely manner. They educated their customers on how to access the system and fill out a request. They also trained their own people, including leaders and project managers, on how to communicate. Basic human interaction skills, such as how to ask questions and handle conflict resolution, are lacking from formal education. Once they addressed both internal and external communications, customer satisfaction went up, employee turnover went down, and the business was able to move into the next phase of growth.

THE GROWTH STAGES OF A BUSINESS

There are seven stages of growth defined by the number of employees. Each stage also comes with its own unique problems. We have an assessment that we do so leaders can see which stage level problems they are dealing with. We go back and show them every stage to highlight those critical building blocks and all the challenges they might have missed.

Every time we share this information, we can see the executives nodding their heads. "We're doing that right now," or "That's exactly what my problem is." If you don't deal with stage one problems in stage one, they will follow you into stages two, three, and four. You don't want to get to stage seven, with more than 160 employees, and still be living in chaos.

The immediate solution is to find subject matter experts in these critical areas like sales, finance, and organizational management. This is a stage four process, and something that is necessary to do as your company grows. Even in stage three, you can be looking forward and hiring the right people that create a productive culture so that you can thrive in stage four.

It's like building blocks. If you don't have the right blocks in your foundation, your structure is going to keep falling. You have to be aware of the challenges in each stage. As a new leader, you might come into your organization at any one of the seven stages. Being aware of the conflicts that each growth stage brings will help you target and resolve the problem. If you are in stage four but still suffering the symptoms of a stage two challenge, you will have to fix that problem first, or your building blocks will fall down around you. I have a quick and easy assessment that will let you see which problems may have been left unaddressed by previous leadership.

SCAN ME : PDF
What Stage Is Your Business or Team In?

FIXED VS. GROWTH MINDSET

Psychologist Carol Dweck in her book " Mindset: The New Psychology of Success" introduced a theory to explain why two students with the exact same challenges could have drastically different final grades in a college class. The key ingredient was mindset. One student believed that a poor initial grade was just a stumbling block and had faith that they would overcome the challenge and rise to the occasion. The second student believed that the poor initial grade was an indication of their intelligence and never did any better. Dweck called these outlooks fixed versus growth mindsets.

"In a fixed mindset, people believe their basic qualities, like their intelligence or talent, are simply fixed traits." (Dweck, 2015) There is no way they are going to increase their intelligence or increase their talent, so there is little use in trying. People with fixed mindsets are not open to new ideas or change. They tend to stay right where they are and view all the rules and social norms as ironclad laws. Most people gravitate towards a fixed mindset when they are under stress. Stress makes it harder to see options and harder to remain optimistic. In a company in crisis, it is typical to find many employees and leaders operating with a fixed mindset.

"In a growth mindset, people believe that their most basic abilities can be developed through dedication and hard work—brains and talent are just the starting point. This view creates a love of learning and a resilience that is essential for great accomplishment." (Dweck, 2015) The student who was able to turn their grade around and exceed expectations despite an early low scoring test had a growth mindset. No company will ever manage to pull itself out of crisis without someone in leadership operating in a growth mindset. As a new leader, one of the most valuable things you can bring to the table is an understanding that things can and will improve.

CHAPTER 6:

IT'S NOT BUSINESS, IT'S PERSONAL

We all know the famous line from *The Godfather:* "It's not personal, Sonny. It's strictly business." Michael Corleone meant that his actions, up to and including murder, had nothing to do with Sonny personally. Sonny could have been the most interesting man in the world, and it wouldn't have mattered. If you've spent any time in business, you know that business *is* personal.

Whether it is a leader interacting with their employee, or an employee interacting with a customer, there is always a personal element to business. Perception, culture, and communication are all ways that we internalize workplace drama. By taking the time to explore each one, we can take the Godfather's claim and flip it around to "It's not business, it's personal."

CHIROPRACTIC COLLEGE IN CONFLICT

Earier in the book I mentioned the chiropractic college I worked with that went from near bankruptcy to international fame. They are a perfect example of personalities influencing business outcomes. There was a civil war going on between the academic staff and the leadership of the college. And there was strife happening internally with the executive team as well.

The first thing we did was to implement behavior assessments. I started with the executive team because they were the voice, the compass, and the standard of the organization. The rest of the school would follow what they did. When they had internal strife, it spilled over into the teams and the departments and everything else. I wanted to get to the bottom of the personal conflict by asking basic questions. Who are you? How are you being perceived? Why do you do what you do?

We came back together as a team after working individually. We asked questions in the group setting such as, "How are we working together?" and "How do we execute knowledge?" When we did the assessment as a team, everyone began to understand who they were in relationship to the organization and why there was conflict. Egos started going off. Now the dean knows why she irritates the CFO, and the CEO understands why a certain process is so important to the IT department. It was a lightbulb moment for the entire executive suite.

After we swept all of that personal information out of the corners and onto the table, we could create a cohesive team that could communicate between different behavior styles.

They understood what motivated their peers, and how different value mechanisms were interacting.

We brought it all back to the mission. We developed objectives. We identified the roles. Once that was clarified, we could move on to the strategy and finally we knew what we were doing and why we were doing it.

The next challenge was to communicate all that to the rest of the organization. The academic camp wanted to slow down. They wanted to analyze everything before making a move in any direction. I sat down for interviews with all the staff, the faculty, and the direct reports. The faculty felt they were losing their legacy. They saw the work that the executive camp was doing, and it frightened them.

I went to a student recruitment event and interviewed a couple of interested students and parents. I asked, "Why are you choosing this college in particular?" Over ninety percent of the answers fell into two categories.

They have a very strong family atmosphere, and

The academics are second to none.

Students felt that this school was more focused on the science of chiropractic practice versus other business topics. Their philosophy was a pure philosophy, and it was attracting people away from other colleges. So, the reality was that the school was not in danger of losing its legacy. The legacy was strong, and the customers were responding.

I took this information to the CEO and made some very specific recommendations. He had to communicate to the academic staff that he was not going to change the legacy. The school should remain grounded in chiropractic science, and it should retain the family atmosphere. Now that we understood why people chose this college, we needed to expand on the strengths. The message to the faculty needed to be that we are not changing the fundamentals, we're actually building on them.

Both the executives and the academics were taking the conflict personally. They each had ideas about the other group that were unfounded. We needed to get in and uncover the unspoken assumptions that each person was making about themselves and their role in the organization in order to move forward. Once we understood the motivation behind the conflict, we could address the real issue and fix the problem. The personal situation was affecting the school's ability to develop a mission, objectives, and roles that would facilitate a return to profitability. Dealing with personal matters allowed us to fix what was broken.

─────

SELF-PERCEPTION

Self-perception is critical in our decision-making processes. Based on how we perceive ourselves, we may be comfortable taking risks or fearful of the consequences. All of us, as human beings, are dealing with three main areas that shape our perception: fears, weaknesses, and insecurities. How you perceive those three things determines your view of yourself. Most of us have felt like we were faking it at some point in time. We are all wearing a mask and we're all pretending to be something we're not. This is especially true for people who have been thrust into a new position, whether by promotion or a new hiring decision.

The old advice, "Fake it till you make it," is addressing just that scenario. We've all felt that way, it doesn't say anything about who you are as a person. The question becomes how do you deal with those insecurities? Do you educate yourself? Allow yourself to try and fail? Or do you continue to wear the mask and hope no one notices?

If you are planning to run from your fears and weaknesses, I have a wake-up call for you. People can tell. We might be able to fool them for a while, but sooner or later, they can always tell. Ultimately, their perception of our authenticity defines our relationship with them.

Leaders I dealt with during the early months of the COVID-19 crisis felt like they were walking around with a brave or optimistic mask on. They couldn't let their employees see how much they were worrying about the bottom line. The lack of information made it difficult to have a plan, but they had to pretend to have direction in order to keep the ship afloat. They decided to fake it and pretend to be clear and strong.

On the employees' side, they were not fooled. People criticized their leadership for not communicating. They didn't understand what was going on and didn't feel like they were getting any clarity from their bosses. They saw right through the charade of competence and understood intrinsically that the leaders didn't have much more information than they did. A better way to handle the situation would have been to have an authentic conversation with the employees.

"Look, we don't know what is going to happen. Based on the information we do have, here is the plan. The plan might change. It might change tomorrow. We'll keep you informed as we go forward." This type of honest communication would have soothed the anxiety much more than pretending to have all the answers.

Self-perception is not always correct. You may see yourself in a certain light, but it is likely that your employees will figure out your true motivations. Taking some time to discover your patterns and motivations will help you effectively manage your team.

CULTURE

Leaders create culture. How we perceive ourselves is dependent on that culture. There are some cultures that give you the ability to be yourself, to innovate, and be in an entrepreneur role. Some cultures stress conformity, and caution everyone to "Stay in their own lane." If you hire the wrong person for the wrong culture, their entire perception of themself turns negative. *I'm not good enough. I don't fit,* they think. They internalize their inability to work within the established culture and start to make artificial changes to try to get along. That's when you get anxiety, depression, and PTSD, because they're trying to do something that they're not naturally capable of doing. They become an imposter. That, in turn, makes them difficult to deal with and drives down productivity for the entire team.

Are you hiring and leading the right people for your particular workplace culture? You need personalities that match because that will create a natural arena for them to thrive. If leaders are not aware of the culture they create, it can have disastrous effects on the bottom line. I have seen top performers leave organizations because they didn't like the corporate culture. People were working in silos, and there was inner team conflict. A toxic culture always points back to the leader and, usually, the leader was never trained. They don't have the skill sets, the emotional caution, or the ability to communicate effectively.

Culture is a powerful influence over everything in the workplace. Employees, teams, customer relations, and even product development can all be swayed by the climate of the office. As a new leader, assessing the workplace culture should be one of your first tasks. If too many people are trying to fit in, or if there is low productivity and a lot of waste, the culture could be to blame. As a leader, you have the power to shape the culture moving forward. By hiring the right people and making roles and responsibilities clear, you can repair relationships and allow everyone to be authentic.

KING-SIZED EATS

One company I worked with went through a struggle that is a perfect example of the business-personal dynamic. I'll call them King-Sized Eats. They were a regional heavy hitter with twenty-five franchises in the Mid-Western market. The CFO was about to get promoted to COO, but he wasn't comfortable in the new role. He was so analytical and that worked well as head of finance. But the COO position came with more personal interaction and management. He wasn't prepared and it showed.

He was a great CFO because he was logical and detail oriented and that was why they thought he would be a great chief operating officer. But the regional managers and the senior executive team were all alphas, not number crunchers. This poor sheep of a CFO was now in charge of wolves, and he was going to get eaten alive. I wish I could have videotaped the first executive meeting because he was so bad. He was trying so hard to be something that he wasn't, and it was pathetic. He was a smart, gentle person, in the wrong environment.

His leadership type was an Influencer. He wanted to get along with everyone and was constantly evaluating whether an action would make him more popular. Logically, he understood that certain things needed to get done, but he was always questioning, "Do they like me? Am I accepted?"

Every human being has needs and fears that drive their decision-making process. These underlying insecurities create our perception of ourselves and the world around us. His fear was that he would not be accepted. He had imposter syndrome; he didn't believe he was good enough for the job. He created a situation in which his personal value was predicated on his employees' opinion, not the work he did.

Everyone saw through him immediately. They wondered, "What the hell is wrong with this guy?" He was brilliant, but because he was pretending to be something he was not, nobody took him seriously. He wasn't connecting with his staff, and everybody knew it. Instead of taking a step back and looking at the cycle he was trapped in, he tried even harder.

He doubled down on it, trying to be everyone's friend, not holding anyone accountable, not having clear communication of goals and objectives. He came across as so fake that the entire productivity of that department sank. That was when I was brought in.

I did what I call a 360-degree assessment, looking at all of his habits, behaviors, and underlying assumptions. I looked at his motivations, his needs, and his fears, and I realized that he had a very poor perception of himself. I sat him down and told him that he wasn't going to succeed at being popular unless he began to trust himself. You cannot validate your actions based on other people's opinions, especially as a new team leader. The reason King-Sized Eats promoted this man was because of the excellent work that he had done as CFO. The problem wasn't that he was lacking in intelligence or education. The problem was that he didn't have the skills and the training necessary to establish himself in the new position.

Once the COO saw what I was talking about, his attitude started to change. He was enthusiastic about the process because it felt manageable. That's always a big hurdle when it comes to making any kind of major change. If the challenge seems too daunting, no one wants to start working on it. But if you can show people that the challenge is, in fact, a reasonable one, people will start to get excited about the potential of the change.

We needed to get all the influential people on the team together so that we could figure out how to start improving things. "What does the new COO need to do to earn your trust both for the organization as a whole and for the team?" I asked.

They gave me some great feedback because this was a conversation they'd already had with each other. They just needed permission to be open and honest with the COO without fear of reprisal. "We're having to pay for things we don't need at our particular franchise," they said. "We're not getting enough training to onboard our new team members." Once we got the team together, we could identify who he really was and pinpoint the value that he brought to the table. That enabled us to figure out what he was doing that was making people uncomfortable. We came up with a plan and a set of mile markers he was going to hit every week.

I chose the top three regional managers and made the COO accountable to them. Every week they were going to give him an honest score on how he did as a leader. Every week we would look at that score together and go over what worked and what didn't. After six weeks of doing this, the team loved the COO, and he was able to make the transition into his new position from a place of authenticity.

Once we become adults, we think we're no longer capable of change, but this is simply not true. With time and genuine effort, we can bring our behaviors back into alignment with our values. That "fakeness" that all his employees were picking up on decreased dramatically because we had established trust. He was willing to fail and to take that constructive criticism. He learned that by trying to be something he was not, he was creating chaos and a toxic work environment.

He was willing to take advice and the entire company saw he was working toward improvement. They became advocates for him with the rest of the team, declaring, "We're going to work with this guy." My client started providing clarity and direction that increased communication and eliminated confusion. As a result, the senior management team performed better and because the team performed better, their franchisees were happier. Once the workplace drama had settled down, they were able to find innovative ways to solve problems that made their franchises more valuable.

As a leader, the concept of open criticism from your staff might be distasteful. You can't ignore the possibility that the problem in the workplace comes from your leadership, especially if you haven't been trained. If you notice you have a cash flow problem, it could be directly related to your internal communication process. It takes guts and humility to set aside your ego for the good of the company. Other people can give you instructions, but if you're not willing to do the work, the exercise becomes disingenuous. At the next meeting, if you show up and make the change they suggested, your employees will see that you are listening. That action will go further than any other incentive in helping to repair broken processes and rescue the bottom line.

Leaders who can recognize that they work for their staff rather than the other way around, have a higher level of self-perception than others. Your job is to facilitate their work, to create an environment and a culture that contains all the tools they need to be productive. Your job is to establish rules and objectives, to hire the right people, and train them well. Your job is *not* to sit back and let the dollars or the praise roll in. Leaders who manage their teams like little fiefdoms will never ensure the loyalty of their personnel. They will be constantly battling employee attrition, lack of enthusiasm, and poor workmanship.

As the leader, your own personal journey is important. Business is personal, and your team needs you to be authentic and clear in your expectations. Don't make the mistake of thinking you can check your fears and insecurities at the door. You have to deal with them if you don't want them to get in the way of productivity.

HOW OTHERS PERCEIVE YOU

How your client perceives you will determine your relationship with them. Nonverbal communication is a tool that allows you to connect, react to, and communicate effectively with anyone you meet. In his book *The Brand Gap,* published in 2003, Marty Neumeier addresses the wide gulf between business strategy and customer experience. Customers don't care about strategy, he argues; they care only about what your product, service, or company means in the context of their lives.

Ultimately, "Your brand isn't what *you* say it is—it's what *they* say it is." Neumeier makes his case and proposes a complete system of brand-building based on the interaction of five disciplines: differentiation, collaboration, innovation, validation, and cultivation. Differentiation involves separating your product from the competition, collaboration is working together within your team, innovation is creative thinking, validation is bringing experts onboard, and cultivation is the act of attracting customers. Each of these strategies goes to the heart of the matter: how to drive perception instead of letting it drive you.

First impressions can dramatically impact a person's chance of success. In those first few seconds, any opportunity to further engage with someone in business, socially, romantically, or professionally can be accelerated or *crushed*. If it's a bad first impression, it could close the door to any chance of further communication.

Nonverbal cues are even more important than the words you use. Like the tuning forks, they emit energy that other people will pick up on subconsciously. In a split second, they will decide whether they like you, trust you, or want nothing to do with you. Rescuing a first impression can be done, as we saw with the COO of King-Sized Eats. But it is much easier to make a good first impression and to carry that through than it is to bounce back from a missed opportunity.

COMMUNICATION

In addition to culture and self-perception, communication is another way we make business personal. There are different methods of communication including speaking, body language, and, increasingly, digital communication. Missing social cues in any of these arenas can lead to lost time and decreased productivity. It could be as simple as speaking English as a foreign language, but there are lots of other reasons why communications fail to connect.

Zoom is just one of the digital platforms we use today to facilitate business meetings. It comes with its own set of social norms; for example, a need to minimize distractions in the background. Many leaders and coworkers are beginning to realize the importance of social skills in the digital landscape. Zoom and other virtual connections create a different form of fatigue that we must identify and adapt to in order to be effective communicators. This is especially important for leaders whose teams are not used to being in a virtual office.

Communication in the beginning of the pandemic was urgent, rushed, and, at best, sparse. By now we have learned how to adapt to the environment and have become more focused. We are getting used to muting and unmuting. We have meeting facilitators and we do not attempt to crowd meetings with hundreds of participants. This means more consistent connection with teams and better communication moving forward. There is also space now for listening and being empathetic to everyone's concerns. Many organizations are actively finding ways to provide calm and clarity.

Before there was virtual communication, before verbal communication even, we communicated through body language. You can observe certain parts of a leader's body, whether it's their eyes, their shoulders, or their hands, and take cues as to the true meaning of their statements. Is the conversation causing stress, or are they excited about it? It's like subconscious engineering, if you will. When we use physical movements to indicate interest, like leaning forward or maintaining eye contact, we can improve communication, which in turn improves performance.

Depending on the personality and motivation involved, you may need to adapt your tone, your pace, or your language so that you can connect. You wouldn't curse around your mother, and yet there are some businesspeople who won't take you seriously if you don't throw in a few curse words. They would interpret that as "stuffy" or "naive" and you would have missed an opportunity to connect. It's all about reading the room. Once you understand behavior, how your employees communicate, and what their fears and needs are, you become a much better leader. Listening and paying attention to behavioral cues will set you up to communicate more effectively.

SCAN ME:
Training Information: How to read anyone in two minutes

Communication to me is similar to engineering discovery principles. How do we take those engineering principles and apply them to human nature? I have been working on a way that we can deconstruct conversation by looking at what you do, what you say, and how you react. We can teach leaders how to adjust and adapt their message to elevate performance. There's often a disconnect between what a leader wants and what is communicated. If standards and expectations aren't clear, the employee will make assumptions. For example, if your company works in Google Docs and shares document links instead of emailing files, making those expectations clear in the onboarding process will save a lot of wasted time and effort.

Once you establish the lines of communication, you can start to grow an awareness, not just about tasks that need to be performed, but also what your company stands for and who its people are. Your team members don't have to know all your deepest darkest secrets, but they must have a sense of who you are and what you value. My job is to get people to open up about what they need. Whether it's a relationship or a work situation, people can be reluctant to ask for help. This is particularly problematic in a work environment because you don't want employees or team members to "fill in the blanks."

You have to *over*communicate, even if it feels ridiculous sometimes. Research suggests that customers need to view an advertisement seven to eight times before they will remember and act on it. Get together with your executive team and nail down your message, then repeat it again and again. The best way to achieve buy-in with your mission and vision is to present it to your team at every opportunity.

In every communication you send, every email or team meeting, make sure you answer the who, what, where, when, and why of each project or task. Even if you have mentioned the deadline before, say it again. Put it in every email; if it's important, don't let your message get lost in a single communication.

As a new leader, you can set the standard for respectful communication in all forms. You can pay attention to the norms of digital meetings and cut down on email clutter by overcommunicating project parameters. You can treat conversations like engineering problems. Break them down to basics, what do you want to accomplish, and what is the best way to communicate? Sometimes a phone call will do, sometimes nothing short of a team meeting will solve the problem. And when communicating in person, pay close attention to your body language. Make sure your hands are sending the same message as your words, or you risk being branded a hypocrite.

TUNING FORKS: HOW WE ALL CONNECT

The room was a ballroom at a hotel in D.C. designed for weddings and corporate gatherings. A massive divider had been drawn shut, cutting the space in half. Rows of chairs faced a podium and a buffet table held not food, but tuning forks. There were twenty of us in the room, participating in a corporate training.

"Come on up and choose a tuning fork." The presenter invited us forward.

I followed my colleagues to the front of the room, then waited my turn to approach the table. The instruments were similar, but not exactly the same. Each was a different size and had a different thickness in the prongs. They were meant to represent the differences between individual styles of communication, each one as unique as the people in the room. I chose a fork and sat back down, holding it in the air.

The presenter picked up one of the last remaining tuning forks and hit it, creating a pitch. Some of the forks in the room rang out, excited by the sound vibrations. Other tuning forks didn't move at all. The presenter repeated the experiment three more times with different tuning forks, and each time different instruments would respond.

"Our energy is picked up by people's brains just like sound waves," the presenter summarized. "Just like the tuning forks, some people will respond well to your frequency, and some people won't. You have to listen first."

The meaning of the exercise was clear. Communication, that skill that has allowed people to collaborate in life as well as in business, is only as good as your tuning fork. As leaders, we must be aware of the vibrations our energy gives off, and its effect on other people. Despite the trend towards robotics and artificial intelligence, there will always be a human component to business. Being an effective leader starts with understanding people and the way their interactions shape their behavior. Listening is a key skill that is unfortunately not taught in school. It's not enough to tap your tuning fork and wait for others to respond. You have to listen for their answering chimes and listen to those who don't reply.

COMMUNICATION IN THE CHIROPRACTIC COLLEGE

The chiropractic school I introduced at the beginning of the book had its own struggles with communication. Each executive had three or four departments and each one of those departments had what's called a "direct report" who functioned as a supervisor. We brought the executive team, the direct reports, and all the faculty into one room and let them hash it out. We had everyone lay out their concerns. We took everything that everyone was feeling and all the unspoken conflict and put it all on the table. That took three days.

I had separated people into pods with six or seven individuals per pod, in a big conference room. We had five sheets of paper and each group had a scribe. The groups went round robin, and each one had a discussion. At the end, we came together and looked for common themes and identified the core of the disagreement. Despite their differing points of view, it became clear that everyone wanted to make sure the students were successful. That was the common theme. I was able to show them, through honest communication, that they had the exact same mission. The passion and drive were the same in both camps, and they both brought necessary components to the picture. The academics had the skills and the knowledge that they were going to pass down to the students, and the executive team had the ability to support the college through increased revenue. It just became a question of how to collaborate.

We came up with a tagline, Focused on Student Success (FOSS) and an entire campaign around that. We had T-shirts that said, "I'm Focused on Student Success Because..." and each person would hand write whatever they wanted in the blank. We added it as a footer to all the college emails. We introduced it in staff meetings and had a few little games to go along with it. And then I started to bridge them together. The academic camp and the executive camp both had a message they could get behind. Through messaging, I helped them see that their common goal outweighed their differences. They began to work together, and that was the key to rescuing the business from declaring bankruptcy.

"IT'S NOT BUSINESS, IT'S PERSONAL"

The reason I chose the title of this chapter is because I wanted to call attention to the common misconception. We think of business as something closer to math. The numbers go up and down and they aren't connected to people or feelings at all. Nothing could be further from the truth. Business is incredibly personal. There are investors whose entire investment strategy is to follow the advice of a trusted acquaintance. Good salespeople know that building a relationship with a potential client is the key to attracting and maintaining their business. A hypocritical leader can drive down productivity when employees lose motivation and trust.

Self-perception is critical in our decision-making processes because it either holds us back from taking risks or enables us to get out there and do our best. Culture dictates how we all interact with each other. There are a lot of different workplace cultures, and I won't say that one is better than another, but you have to pay attention to the people that you hire and make sure they are a good fit.

Communication is important to get everyone on the same page. A new leader has to use all the communication tools available, from virtual meeting software to one-on-one conversations. Above all, communication has to be honest, and body language has to convey the same meaning as the words we use. Because business is personal, we have to take the time to understand our communication, our culture, and our perception. It's not like math where you can plug the same numbers in and get the same answer every time. Business is dependent on people, and people require honesty, trust, and information. If you keep those three things in mind in all your communications with your team, you will be able to meet any challenge the world throws at you.

CHAPTER 7:

LESSONS FROM T-REX: ADAPT OR DIE

STORMING IN THE CHIROPRACTIC COLLEGE

We saw how communication and perception affected the chiropractic college. Let's take a moment to discuss the process that they went through to arrive at their compromise. There are four pillars of adapting, and the one that had the staff trapped in conflict is called "storming." Imagine you are on a team that is doing the same thing day in and day out. Everyone's comfortable. Everyone understands the outcome. And then you throw something new at them. Anxiety goes up and productivity goes down.

The executive team in the chiropractic college did this exact thing to the academic staff by introducing direct reports to serve as the bridge between the faculty and the administration. When the new leader was hired, one of the first things he did was restructure the organizational chart. He reasoned that by adding this layer of the direct reports, he could better facilitate communications throughout the college. But the academic staff didn't see it that way.

There wasn't an organized effort to communicate with the academic staff, so everyone was left alone to decide for themselves the meaning of this structural change. The moment the decision was made, and the direct reports were established, the academic staff started to complain. Communication broke down, and no one was talking to anyone else.

When I walked in, there was no trust, and there were high levels of conflict. Everyone was operating in silos, as if they had their own mini fortresses. No one wanted to take accountability for anything, and productivity plummeted. They were about to close their doors.

I looked at all the players and at their motivations. The academic staff had been there for twenty, thirty, or forty years. They wanted to go back to the way things used to be when the college was well attended and there wasn't so much competition from online universities. The changes that the executive team were making scared them; they wanted to move at a slower pace. They wanted more information before they made any decisions; they wanted data, studies, and surveys. The new leader was an entrepreneur who was figuring things out as he went, trying to change the entire university as necessary without addressing the concerns of identity and legacy.

They both had physiological needs to address and were both ultimately interested in the success of the college. I had a sit down with the CEO and told him, "We need to change the narrative—not the results, but the narrative—and create a bridge to the future without losing the legacy that made this school great." I let that sink in, then continued. "You're not bringing the academics along with you. These are people that you really need to make all of this work."

Once we started to hold those meetings and put things on the table, we were able to collaborate. We built trust and an understanding that it was okay to have constructive conflict and different ideas. Eventually, one of the things I did was to create an idea greater than either of the parties, the FOSS that brought them all together.

When you have a disparity of ideas, you have to recognize that both sides have great points. Your job as a leader is to figure out how each opinion moves you closer to your goal. There were ideas about increasing tuition, bringing more staff onboard, and increasing the quality of the program. Those were things everyone agreed on. We just needed to address the physiological impact of each of those decisions. Would increasing tuition affect the legacy? Would it increase the bottom line, or would it drive students away? We needed action items to get us to our first stage.

They needed fifty more students in the next six months. They needed to increase the staff to provide more educational opportunities and more classes. They needed to pass certification. All of these problems and conflicts created what is called a "storm." Instead of business as usual, the school was thrown into a situation where they had to act, and yet no one agreed on how that should be done. The CEO was making decisions that he felt would benefit enrollment, but without the buy-in from the academic staff. That only increased the stormy environment because more than half of the staff felt that their needs were not being taken into consideration.

By the time I was done working with them, I had helped them move through the storm into the next two phases of adapting: norming and performing. After we hashed out grievances, there was a new standard of fluid conversation. The executive team would make a decision that was collaborated by the direct reports, and the direct reports pushed the action downward and made sure that the academic staff were on board. Everyone agreed on a process, or at least understood the methodology behind the process before it was implemented. Once they got rid of the confusion and conflict through communication, there was a workable process.

They built that consistent conversation, holding each other accountable as a collective. It was that common goal, the FOSS, that really made the difference. After that, they were able to work together, surviving, growing, and thriving, all because they believed in the message. The pillars of adapting are standard processes that every organization has to work through when something changes. If, like the chiropractic college, you can come together and design a strategy, then you can pass through each level to emerge productive at the end. Sometimes companies get stuck in the "storming" phase and look to experts such as me for help. Without trust and without your team's buy-in, it is easy to get trapped in chaos and misunderstanding. As a new leader, you have to open the channels of communication to get your entire team on the same page. Only then can you hope to move through the four stages to the end result which is "performing."

FOUR PILLARS OF ADAPTING

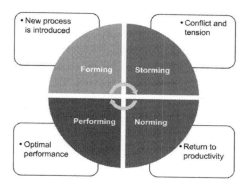

I find that most companies are simply not prepared for the dysfunction that is inevitable in business. They seem to think that they can ignore these challenges by pretending they are immune. This is a shortsighted way of running a company because conflict is inevitable and knowing how to deal with it will give you an edge over the competition.

Notorious boxing champ Mike Tyson was fond of saying, "Everyone's got a plan until they get hit." While he may have been bragging about the power of his own punches, he was right on the money about expectations versus obstacles.

As a new leader, you may have been brought in to address challenges that are already entrenched. Your company had a plan that was working—perhaps even for years—until it suddenly wasn't. Market shifts, new employees, even natural disasters can cause chaos in a normally high-functioning organization. A go-to response from board members and owners is to change management, adding more heat to an already boiling pot.

Most companies fall into a routine, usually based on their culture and how they operate on a day-to-day basis. This routine becomes a source of comfort because it is predictable, and its very predictability can make it hard to escape. Just because something has worked in the past, doesn't mean it will work under different market conditions. Take a look at Blockbuster, a giant in the home movie rental business until the market dried up.

Conflict will affect your company, whether it comes from shifting customer demands or internal politics. There are four distinct stages your organization must work through in order to deal with uncertainty. Forming, storming, norming, and performing provide a framework for savvy leaders to understand the dynamics of change. The process starts with "forming" and the introduction of any new element.

SCAN ME: YouTube Video
Four Pillars of Adapting

FORMING

Most organizations have a routine, a culture, and a comfortable way of doing things. When you introduce something new into that culture, that moves the company into a process called *forming*. Anything that disrupts their comfort zone—whether it is a new person, a new product, or even a new pricing structure—the company must now adapt to. You're moving forward into the unknown when you introduce something new, and employees get scared. They start to ask themselves, "Why was this done, and how does it fit? And how will it affect me?"

The first response for many people when something like this happens is to default to fear. I recently worked with a company that had already worked its way through a complex problem involving the rollout of a new software. They had taken a step back and given everyone the time and the training to learn the new system and get comfortable with the way it operated. They had just weathered the storming phase, and things were looking really good for them. Until COVID-19 hit...

Instead of emerging from crisis and looking forward to a productive year in the performing phase, this company was yanked right back to the forming phase. To get through the pandemic and related shutdowns, they were going to have to "form" into something new. It was a massive disruption to their culture.

A common problem is that the executives at the top see the big picture without considering how the introduction of a new idea will create disruption. A new software system might streamline automation, or might make keeping track of work orders easier, but the staff will have anxiety. That will trickle down to every aspect of the company, including customer relations. The executives see the value in what they're doing but fail to consider the time and energy it will take to move the staff through the four levels of adapting.

When a change like this starts happening, it causes individuals to revert back to their physical needs. Will this affect my ability to acquire food and afford my home? Will I be able to pay my bills? The forming stage leads right into the storming phase because the delicate balance that allowed employees to predict their day-to-day lives has now been thrown out of whack. There is nothing you can do as a leader to prevent the anxiety. Your task is to move the company or your department through the stages as quickly as possible, so that you can get back to performing naturally.

If you're going to introduce something new, you have to provide the right communication. Leaders need to think about the domino effect of their actions and get input as well as buy-in before they introduce a new plan. You need a communication strategy based on information gathered through team meetings and phone calls, not just what you assume people want to hear.

STORMING

The intense, emotional reaction to the introduction of a new process throws a company into "storming." We conducted a study with thousands of companies and found there were three basic components of a storm: conflict, cash flow, and confusion.

Whenever you add something new that disrupts the norm, it creates conflict. And whenever there's conflict, it affects cash flow. When cash flow is affected, there's confusion and often panic. The trick is to recognize the process of storming before it becomes entrenched.

Storming is natural and it won't spell doom for your company unless you leave it unaddressed. If there is a problem with cash flow, maybe due to too many late customer payments, that can cause a storm. As a leader, you need to figure out the root cause, communicate a plan to your entire team, and move your people on to the next stage. If there is confusion, the easiest way to deal with that is through overcommunication. If the problem is conflict, you may have to sit your entire team down and get them to talk about the underlying issue. Whatever the solution, your journey starts with recognizing that your team is reacting to the introduction of some uncertainty.

New leaders struggle with taking a step back to identify what caused the storm before they attempt to right the ship. This can look like micromanaging, making erratic decisions, or blaming other people. They are so focused on fixing the problem that they fail to see that they are creating a bigger issue. Micromanaging creates a toxic work environment, by insinuating that you don't trust your team members. Too many pivots when solutions don't work will leave employees fatigued and frustrated. Figuring out who is at fault usually doesn't help resolve the problem at hand.

Another way leaders may unknowingly create a storm is by not considering the ripple effect of change or how best to communicate it. For example, an email goes out about a new hire, or a price change on a product, or worse, a delay in production. All of these create conflict in two ways, the method of communication (email rather than face-to-face) and a lack of strategy to overcome or mitigate the change. Leaders should work with their teams and speak with them in person when any new change or deviation of their current process is about to be made. This will help the team to understand, feel respected, and be part of the conversation. Otherwise, they will feel blindsided and began to create the *"what if"* conflict in their mind.

The typical response to the storming phase is a desire to get back to normal as quickly as possible. It is hard to see what is coming next and how the team will survive this phase. The emotional part of the brain is overreacting to the potential loss of whatever normal thing has been replaced, whether it is a well-known software system or a familiar colleague. In the storming phase, people are not thinking about the opportunity for gain.

We have all been there in one situation or another. You go for a road trip, and you take the wrong exit. Suddenly, you cannot find a way onto the highway. Your brain panics, feeding you scenarios in which you drive hopelessly for hours through cornfields and possibly run out of gas. We have all had that feeling of, "Crap, what do I do now?" We want our "normal" back as quickly as possible.

New leaders need to collaborate with their teams on how to integrate changes into their process and continue to execute effectively. The problem I see too often is that companies don't even know that they're in the middle of a storm because they're trying desperately to act as though everything is normal. Blockbuster ignored the approaching market shift and doubled down on their offerings of candy and popcorn at the register. They believed that their model of providing a Friday night "activity" by forcing customers to come to them would withstand the innovation of Netflix's home streaming platform. Ignoring the new element caused them to close store after store and eventually become a cautionary tale rather than a thriving business.

Storming is a process of chaos and confusion brought on by the introduction of a new element in the forming stage. Storming almost always affects cash flow and involves conflict both internally and externally. Since storming is the most volatile stage of the adapting process, let's take a closer look at how you can move your team out of this stage. Until you take the necessary steps, you're going to find yourself trapped in a perpetual cycle between storming and forming. Trying to introduce something new to fix the problem will only perpetuate the cycle, creating more of the same conflict.

THREE KEYS TO OVERCOMING THE STORM: CLARITY, PROCESS, AND COMMUNICATION

If you were brought in to lead your team out of a storm, your first plan of attack should be **communication**. Gather all the information you need to know first, including what that new thing was that drove people to a state of panic. Talking to a few key stakeholders should allow you to understand what the workplace was like before the storm and how it is reacting after.

You need to develop a clear methodology or process for why and how you will take action. There isn't a right way or a wrong way, but you can't go off by yourself and develop a plan without checking with your team first. They need to feel like they are a part of the process. It's also important to communicate to your customers because you are introducing something new to the market. If they don't have a good understanding of *why* this change is happening, it throws everyone back into that cycle of anxiety.

This kind of communication where everyone, from the employees to the customer, understands the goal, is what gets you out of the storm and into the norming phase. During my time in the Marines, we would make sure every soldier understood the mission, the objective, and their part in the overall plan before marching out. That way, when the unexpected happened, we could remain on task and complete the mission.

Occasionally, leaders have to have difficult conversations, and the likelihood that you will have to discipline or fire someone increases during a storm. How do you have difficult conversations, especially if you don't like conflict? How can you improve your skills in breaking bad news when there is so much riding on your ability to do so? Often, when we do assessments, we see that people are struggling to remain in positions that aren't really suited to them. It could be that a problem employee is well educated and charismatic, they just don't fit into their current role.

Having a difficult conversation with them could then become an exercise in helping them move into a position that is more suited for them. You don't have to stress their bad qualities or dwell on why there is conflict with other team members. If you put the stress on finding the right situation for them, either through additional training, moving to a different department, or maybe separating from the company altogether, the conversation will be smoother. You may not know where they truly belong, but if you approach the dialog as if trying to help them figure out where they do fit, that conversation may be easier to have.

Clear communication answers the questions "What are we doing? And why are we doing it?" Poor cash flow is an uncomfortable position for any company to be in, and helping people process the crisis so that they can clearly see their alternatives comes down to **clarity**. By setting simple standards and expectations for your team, you can cut through the panic that storming creates.

"Here's what we're doing," you need to say. "This is our goal, and this is what everyone is going to do to get us there." By giving your team clarity of direction and purpose, by defining roles and responsibilities, you can un-muddy the waters. You can bring everyone back to the table with a structure in place that will keep the process moving.

Process is the third strategy that will help you overcome the storm. Companies who understand that they will face the storming phase have already created a plan. "If we're going to introduce something new," they realize, "we have to provide the right communication." So maybe they have a process to move their people through to the next stage of adapting. Ordinarily, though, companies are not so up to speed on behavioral theory.

Process is like a game plan that will move you and your employees forward. It includes tools such as communication, mission, and vision. It lays out a path for you to follow and helps everyone get on board. If you communicate your process effectively, employees, customers, and managers will know what is expected of them and what they can expect from you.

Once you're clear about the process and you communicate that in a manner that everyone understands, you can move into the "norming" phase of adapting. Even if you only manage one department, you can transition your team to the norming phase inside of the larger company storm. Look at the healthcare industry and the linen company story from Chapter 1. The entire industry was in crisis due to the pandemic and the increase in the number of hospitalizations worldwide. Yet, the linen company was able to innovate within that storm and create a process that cut down on confusion.

SPARKPRO

Here is an extreme example of an executive team who threw their company into the storming phase, and the incredible amount of work it took to pull them out. They eventually used clear communication and an agreed-upon process to bring all of their employees on board. When I heard what they were planning to do, I was shocked. I could just imagine the level of panic and chaos they were unleashing, but I was unable to stop it.

"We're releasing SparkPro globally on Tuesday," the CEO told me. SparkPro is a made-up name for the well-known software suite they were going to install.

I couldn't even say anything. I was stunned. "Wait a minute, have you done small tests in independent markets?" They had an archaic system that ran their entire corporation from HR through supply ordering.

He said, "No, we're just going to roll it out and as things come in, we'll fix them."

"I hope you don't plan on doing anything for the next eight months." He thought I was joking, but it was actual fact. "This is all you're going to do. Do you understand the ripple effect of this?"

"Don't worry about it," he assured me.

They released in December, and I got a phone call three weeks later saying, "My world is imploding!"

I had tried to explain this to him. Not only was he introducing something without getting feedback, insight, and ownership from the teams, but he was doing it across different nations. That is the very definition of a storm. The employees were panicking and were worried about their paychecks. Cash flow and productivity dropped. The salespeople couldn't connect with the customers because they were having a hard time learning how to use this new software. There were bugs in the rollout, just like there always are with new systems, which created confusion.

They did not think about the ripple effect of any of this. All they saw was a new toy. I had to help them develop a process to train the employees to work out the bugs in the new system and help the customers connect with their representatives. We had a communication campaign that involved several livestreamed meetings, dedicated email blasts, and paid training. It took a lot of effort to bring the staff around to a place where they were able to use the new system like normal. The moral of the story is: Don't ever underestimate the magnitude of the storm.

NORMING

Once you are finally through storming, the next phase is "norming." In this phase, things are functioning well, as they should. They still need you there as a leader, especially if you are the one who rescued them from the storm. But your team should be able to function efficiently without too much of your attention. In the norming phase, leaders are mentoring and attending to cultural development. You're guiding, but you no longer have to be out front.

You will know that you've reached this stage when you find that the conflict has been resolved. You can continue the same level of clear communication, but there is not the same urgency as there was before. You can turn your attention to the future, and the three-year or five-year plan. Cash flow should have rebounded, and employees are no longer fixated on where their next paycheck is coming from.

PERFORMING

The final stage of adapting is "performing." In this stage, your team is functioning so well that you don't even need to be there. They have the ability to manage conflict on their own, and you trust their judgement should anything unplanned occur. If you have managed to steer your team all the way to the performing stage, take a vacation. You can be lying on a beach in Jamaica and things will still run smoothly. For many leaders, this is the ultimate goal. They can focus their attention on another venture because they don't feel the need to babysit the original organization.

What truly makes a competent leader is that they trust the process. They understand they have to go through a storm, but at the end it is going to be better for everyone. There are four distinct phases to look for and established ways to bring your organization out of each phase. If your intent is to help everyone, by introducing something new, be aware of this process and be proactive about moving your staff through. You have to get buy-in. You have to listen and communicate clearly. You may not be able to avoid change, but you don't have to let it cause the downfall of your entire company.

MASLOW'S HIERARCHY

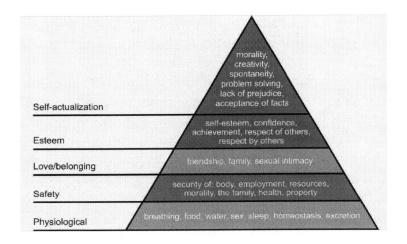

Through each chapter in this book, you will see that there is a common theme. As new leaders, the better you get at people skills, the more effective you will become at developing trust, teamwork, effective communication, and the ability to influence better performance. In previous chapters, we spoke about what drives and motivates an organization. In this chapter, I want to go deeper into the understanding of what drives people to do what they do. This will be very helpful for new leaders especially when training, making changes, and facing those difficult conversations we all dread. With a better understanding of the human evolutionary drivers that dictate our perceptions and our needs, you will gain a different perspective of those around you that will elevate your skill as an effective communicator and leader.

Abraham Howard Maslow developed a theory to explain the motivations that every person brings to every situation.

Understanding Maslow's Hierarchy of Needs can help you navigate conflict and address issues before they derail your company. Maslow discovered five categories of needs that everyone has to meet, in order: physiological needs, safety needs, love and belonging, self-esteem, and self-actualization. Since all of us experience these same drives regardless of age, gender, or culture, I'd like to introduce them briefly and talk about what they mean for your organization.

Physiological needs are breathing, food, water, sex, sleep, and all the things that the body has to have in order to stay alive. You could even include Wi-Fi and social media in the list here because people are that attached to their devices. Every human being requires that these needs be met before they can consider moving on to the next level. They become the primary focus above all other things. If you are hungry, you might risk traversing a minefield for a loaf of bread. That's the hierarchy of needs in effect. Hunger is more important than safety.

Once your basic physiological needs are met, you can consider your environment: employment, resources, property, and health. All of these considerations come under the umbrella of safety. When your job is threatened, you could lose your home or your ability to provide food for your family. The job is a safety net that keeps you from falling into homelessness. Whenever you threaten an employee's paycheck, whether deliberately or by accident, that person's thoughts will go straight to concerns of safety. This is why the organizational storms that we described in the previous chapter occur.

It's not about the money, it's about Maslow's Hierarchy of Needs. The loss of a job indicates a loss of safety, and that is a basic need. When a company is in the storming phase and you've introduced something new, that disrupts the staff's sense of security. Suddenly, they are focused not on productivity, but on making sure those basic needs are met. It starts to affect their interaction with the organization and the team. Helping people move past their panic starts with identifying which needs are unmet and helping team members achieve those goals. The company Gravity Payments lowered anxiety by giving their entire staff a pay raise. If that is out of the question, you could find other ways to address the unmet needs, such as severance packages or tuition reimbursement benefits.

Love and belonging are the next tier in Maslow's Hierarchy. This is where workplace culture comes in. People want to belong; it is our nature as social animals. In a tribe, even if you fall, the tribe picks you up and supports you. You want every employee to fit into the workplace culture so that they can be supported and encouraged by their peers. When you hire the wrong personality type or promote the wrong person into the wrong team, you are interfering with that need for belonging.

When all three of these needs are met, an employee can move on to focus on their level of self-esteem and confidence. They can be a productive member of the team, freely sharing ideas and creativity in their workspace. Everyone needs to feel good about themselves, but that can only happen when the first three basic needs are met. People in this stage are not afraid, and they are ready to devote their energy to team projects. They are willing to have honest conversations and are committed to moving the company forward.

As a new leader, it helps to be aware of the delicate balance of productivity and how it can be influenced by unmet needs. I've seen tragic situations where salespeople were redistributed away from territories they've had for twenty years. Suddenly, all their familiar clients are handed off to someone new. And now that person has to learn an entirely new location with new clients and different traffic patterns. That manager just took someone who was operating at a level four with all their basic needs met to someone who was struggling with concerns of safety.

The apex of the pyramid is self-actualization. At this level, you might have staff members working on their master's or doctoral degrees. People might learn a new language or a new sport, whatever it takes for them to broaden their horizons. With all the basic needs met, people still have a desire to become better versions of themselves. High achievers in the workplace might take on new responsibilities or sign up for tasks just to gain new experiences.

What is important to understand about this hierarchy is that all of these steps are connected, and they all affect one another. Whether we know it or not, most of us spend our lives trying to climb this pyramid because on some level we know that getting to the top will bring us the satisfaction that we all crave.

Understanding that we all naturally move up and down the pyramid will help you see your teammates, employees, and even clients from a different perspective. When you take a step back and look at the situation from the hierarchy pyramid, you can ask, "Where are they right now on that pyramid? What is it that they are afraid of losing?" This will help you to have more empathetic conversations and find solutions that have an impact. This is also a great way to motivate your team.

Understanding where they are on the pyramid today and how it correlates to why they are at work, will give you better leverage to make adjustments.

Example:

Your new hire is single, it is their first real job, and they are living with three roommates to save money. This person may be in the middle of tiers one and two on Maslow's Hierarchy of Needs. When you ask them what it is they hope to accomplish for themselves with this job, they might say, "To find my own apartment." Achieving that goal would move them into tier two.

You might continue the conversation with, "I think we can help you with that. Have you picked out a place yet?"

New Hire: Yes

You: How much will your new rent be with all the expenses?

New Hire: $1,850 a month.

You: Okay, let's call it $2,000. How soon can you move into your new apartment?

New Hire: My current lease expires in six months.

You: Let's create a plan to help you meet weekly goals so you can afford that new apartment in six months. How does that sound?

Now you have focused on helping this person transition comfortably into tier two because to that person, that is the most important thing in their lives. When you attach organizational needs to a way to accomplish personal goals, they will be both motivated and focused. It is a win-win.

FEAR-BASED MANAGEMENT

Decisions you make as a leader have a direct effect on your employees. By creating a culture of fear, you are cutting them off at the knees. Employees who are operating from a constant unmet need for safety will not be as creative or productive as they would be if you took steps to remove their anxiety. Fear based leadership moves employees down the pyramid creating a self-preservation need versus a team-based one. In the following example, the vice president of a casino thought she was motivating them when, in reality, she was forcing them to revert to their basic fears.

A large and well known casino in Las Vegas hired me to work with the sales team to improve their ability to go from transactional to relational by teaching them how to communicate and build relationship with clients from around the world. In this particular training, the said vice president of the department sat in and participated in the training. We walked through a specific element of business development, and I explained how each person has their own role. Each individual will bring something to the table, whether it's creativity or organization.

She piped up and said, "Well, they know that if they can't deliver on a quarterly basis, they're fired." She had explained that to every single one of her employees when they were first hired.

I don't like bullies, so I said, "That's probably the reason your competition is eating you for lunch. Your clients see that fear in your salesperson's approach and therefore they don't feel comfortable. I pulled her aside and told her, "The problem may not be the sales process in itself, it may be the team's perception and response as to how the leadership is holding them accountable."

She was stunned. As we debriefed in her office after the traning, she explained that she never saw it that way before. She had thought it was just a business transaction, never bothering to consider what that fear did to her bottom line. I had recorded the meeting and I played it back for her.

"I don't want you to listen to what you said," I explained. "I want you to focus on the faces of everyone else in the room after you said it."

We watched the video, and you could see the petrified looks and the tension and anxiety on every one of those faces, including the executives. "You can either be that charismatic leader who inspires them to success, or Attila the Hun," I said. "And right now, you're leading by fear. And that fear is what is driving the team and affecting your ability to be relational with your clients. Their priority diverted from building relationships, value and trust into "do what ever it takes to meet the numbers so I won't loose my job."

Her actions had caused all the salespeople to revert to their basic need for safety. They couldn't have the open and honest conversations they needed to have in order to forge working relationships with their clients. I showed her Maslow's Hierarchy and explained what her ultimatum was doing to her staff. At times we just don't know what we don't know. Once she understood how her actions, words, and comfort zone were sending mix messages, she quickly made some adjustments. She began to work with her leaders to use the assessment for each team member in order to improve her approach and accountability process and to better reflect the key performance indicators (KPIs) that were not just financial in nature. These actions translated into greater sales, happier teams, and more engaged employees.

LESSONS FROM T-REX

The T-Rex, like all the dinosaurs, is a thing of the past. If you allow your company to get caught in the storm by refusing to communicate or ignoring conflict, you risk becoming extinct like the dinosaurs. We don't even have to go back as far as the Jurassic Period to see evidence of companies making poor decisions.

In recent years, many industry giants have gone under, unable to survive the online marketplace. Sears, Kodak, Blockbuster, Toys R US and Circuit City are just a few notable companies that went the way of the T-Rex. By helping your company through the storm and by recognizing when your employees have unmet needs, you can make sure that you'll be around for years to come. As a new leader, you are in a great position to have a positive influence on systems and departments that may need rapid repair. You can use behavioral science to fix broken communication and calm the panic caused by disruption.

CHAPTER 8:

DYSFUNCTION COMES IN ALL COLORS

FIVE DYSFUNCTIONS

In the book *Five Dysfunctions of a Team,* author Patrick Lencioni establishes five ways that teams go wrong. I introduce these concepts to help my clients understand and avoid typical pitfalls. Absence of trust, fear of conflict, lack of commitment, avoidance of accountability, and inattention to results are the roadblocks that will prevent your team from performing well. Let's take a look at each one and how important they are to your ultimate success.

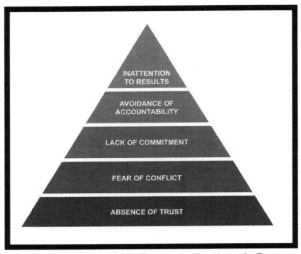

Source: Patrick Lencioni's The Five Dysfunctions of a Team

ABSENCE OF TRUST

Absence of trust is the first and most pervasive dysfunction. When those psychological safety needs are not met, it creates a lack of trust in the entire environment. Maslow's Hierarchy states that safety needs have to be met before self-actualization can occur. In order for people to perform at their best, they need to trust that their more immediate needs will be met. If they are worried about losing their jobs, Just like the example earlier about a casino, that fear becomes all consuming. But when we talk about team performance, it goes a little bit deeper.

The reason there's a lack of trust is because there's no sense of vulnerability. People tend to protect themselves by shielding their true wants and desires from the outside world. When you don't have trust in other people, you're less likely to be vulnerable. Without vulnerability, no one can be authentic. Without authenticity, the free exchange of ideas is stifled, and the workplace becomes less innovative.

Leaders have to set the tone in their own environment, especially new leaders or leaders of newly created teams. In the storming phase, there is a lot of conflict. People have to be able to trust the process, trust each other, and trust themselves. Your newest team member, straight out of school, may have a brilliant idea. But if there is an absence of trust, and they don't believe in their own abilities, that idea may never see the light of day. As a leader, you need to model vulnerability to get your team to open up.

Doc Rivers, head coach of the LA Clippers in 2014, modeled vulnerability to great effect. When Donald Sterling, owner of the LA Clippers, was caught on tape making racist remarks to his girlfriend in 2014, the entire industry was up in arms. Doc Rivers was the first to make a statement to this team. Instead of just condemning the hate speech, he explained how he was feeling. He was vulnerable, and he showed how there was power in that vulnerability. He also respected and never discounted how others were feeling, even if others felt different at the moment. He spoke the truth as he saw it, encouraging others to be better by example.

Especially at such a high level, with the attention of the national media and billions of dollars at stake, being vulnerable can seem like a risky decision. In fact, it is the only thing that will bring people together. Most managers and ineffective leaders want to appear tough. They don't want to share their feelings or discuss how negative stereotypes affect them and their careers. People worry about losing authority and imagine that respect comes from embodying an idealized image of success. But at the end of the day, we are all people, and most people will respect honesty more than the illusion of perfection.

When there is no trust or vulnerability, people become hesitant to communicate their true feelings. This results in what we call artificial harmony. People are determined to get along, even if the camaraderie is disingenuous. Team members stab each other in the back or talk about each other, all while maintaining a friendly façade.

As a leader, you have to be the first one to set the tone. You have to establish what vulnerability means within your company. Are you creating a safe place for your employees not only to trust each other, but to feel comfortable articulating their concerns? Are you rewarding honesty, or are you forcing people to play a role that they may not be comfortable playing?

TRUST IN THE MILITARY

The military develops trust within teams with remarkable precision. They put soldiers in situations where they live, breathe, play, and work next to each other because lives are on the line. You have to be able to trust your teammates. There are split-second decisions in which high performance makes the difference between life and death. There is no room for posturing or pretending to have skills you don't have.

In combat situations, each person's innate abilities come out very quickly. If someone is not comfortable performing a certain task, it becomes obvious and will interfere with the mission if it is not addressed. A military leader has body bags to think about, and other people's safety both on the battlefield and back home. It's an extreme situation that you may not experience, but if you consider the stakes of your own enterprise, there are some parallels. Failure to meet third quarter profits may not send young recruits home in caskets, but you are responsible for metaphorical body bags. Employees' livelihoods, their mortgages, their kids' colleges, their futures, and their dreams all rest in your hands.

It is up to you and how you lead to ensure that these things are protected rather than destroyed. If you don't provide for them, employees could literally find themselves jobless. That security net is only there if you create it. The team has to come first, not your ego, not your year-to-date expenses, not who is right, or who is wrong. None of that stuff matters if you're leaving team members behind. When it comes to dysfunction of a team, they have to be able to trust that their leader has their back, otherwise the mission will be in jeopardy. As a leader, you need to figure out quickly what kind of example you are going to set and be that person.

I led my team through a confusing combat situation by being honest and encouraging. We had one guy in what's called a forward observer, which is a big hole in the ground that we dig for cover. Imagine a hole about six feet wide, about six feet deep to stand up in so that if someone throws a grenade, you'll be protected. When you're in combat, you can't stand up or you'll draw enemy fire. So, we use these forward observing pits, which are deep enough for the average person to stand in.

I had one guy in the forward observing post, and I was crawling over to him to make sure he was okay. The radio was clear; that was important. I was to the right, one of my guys was to the left, the other guy was going back to get something to eat. I leaned over to the guy in the hole to make sure he was clear. He understood what the signal was. And as I turned over, I saw an explosion of dirt. One of the rounds from the enemy would have hit him if his head hadn't turned to look at me.

So now everyone in the pit was panicking. I was on the radio, "Receiving fire?" "Confirm direction." We had scouts with binoculars, looking at everything that was happening. They had a better vantage point, and I needed intel from them.

They said, "Stand down." "Eyes on target," meaning the snipers had the target in their sights.

In the middle of battle, things get confusing. You can have friends firing on friends because they can't see what's going on. It can be hard to distinguish from enemy fire, but with lives on the line, we want to make sure our reaction is appropriate. What the scout was telling us was that somebody fired on us.

We came that close to an international incident. If we had reacted without stopping to evaluate the situation, we could have caused casualties among our allies. It was a powder keg. If you think there's pressure in the board room, imagine a live combat situation in which you can't tell who is firing at you. One miscommunication and not only would we have had an international incident on our hands, but we would have turned our friends into mortal enemies and then had a combined force of hundreds of people with weapons and a reason to shoot at us.

In that situation, I calmed my team down, telling them to take cover and wait it out. The friendly fire ceased, and at that time, no one was injured. We avoided escalating the situation by getting on the phone as quickly as possible and reaching out to our scouts to gain clarity of the situation and to communicate the facts of the current situation. They, in turn, provided information to us as quickly as we needed it, helping us to understand what was happening.

Trust was essential in this situation. An outsider can have a better grasp of the big picture because he can see all the moving parts and provide a logical assessment of the situation. I had to trust my scouts; my team had to trust me. We all needed to trust that the system would work as we expected it to, and that everyone would perform well under pressure. In the absence of trust, any number of tragedies could have occurred. People could have overreacted and died, and the incident could have provoked a much larger conflict. Trust was what got us through to the other side safely. As a next generation leader, it is up to you to model trust and to put it into practice no matter what the stakes.

By willing to be first and establishing that respecting each other's point of view, vulnerability, openness, and honesty are acceptable, you create a standard. Employees will understand that it is okay to have difficult conversations and that their issues can be addressed for the empowerment of the team. Trust helps solve many issues that can keep you from performing efficiently as a team.

FEAR OF CONFLICT

The next most common team dysfunction is fear of conflict. It may seem counterintuitive, but you want your team to be able to disagree. A lot of people have a natural inclination to avoid conflict. They see it as stressful, and there needs to be a level of vulnerability before people are willing to make their feelings known. Without conflict, you won't get the best product or the best process. People will "go along to get along," and innovation will suffer. This is why the foundation that avoids team conflict is **trust**.

Of course, you don't want conflict that will stagnate your process, but you do want healthy conflict. People need to be able to express their opinions and disagree with each other. Without trust and authenticity, team members are hesitant to be their true selves. When that hesitancy exists, they are more likely to avoid conflict affecting innovation, new ideas, and growth.

As a team member or a manager, you might discover another type of conflict avoidance: passive-aggressive behavior. Others may try to derail your career by pointing out your flaws or sabotaging your plans, and they will try to use your carcass to step up to the next rung. The solution goes back to communication. Typically, I will see managers have these quarterly meetings sometimes for three or four hours and the only vision and voice you hear is their own. That type of communication is irrelevant. What are they accomplishing? An effective leader breaks things down and gets input from their team much more often.

You need to set critical milestones for the period but communicate around those milestones every week. Reevaluate your goals as you go. If you have done the first step right, and have achieved vulnerability within your team, that should also mitigate a lot of the backstabbing. As a leader, you also want to set a "door is always open" policy. If something is going sideways or a team member feels that something doesn't work, they will be willing to let you know sooner rather than later.

FEAR OF CONFLICT IN THE MILITARY

Conflict and the military go hand-in-hand. You wouldn't think that the armed forces would suffer from the same dysfunctions as corporate teams, but you would be wrong. I worked with a group of new recruits once at a hotel in a combat zone. We had two factions in this country fighting each other. There were three strategic buildings in play: an airstrip, the hotel, and the embassy. At the airstrip, one faction was camped out, fighting the people in the hotel. We were about 200 yards behind the fighting, closer to the ocean. The embassy was maybe three or four blocks down the road, and we were protecting the diplomats who were trying to escape.

As we were evacuating, a missile came out of the hotel, heading not towards the airstrip, but to the ocean behind us. We barely missed being blown to bits. So, the pucker factor goes way up. A pucker factor is a military slang to describe the level of stress response to a crisis. Every leader at the same time goes "Who was it? What do we do?" And it was "Hold, hold, hold." If the guys in the hotel were shooting at us, we had to take cover, we had to respond, and we had to protect the diplomats in our care. But if the missile had been a mistake, then we would need to resume our mission and get the people to safety ASAP. We had to define the combat fire first in order to know how to react.

This is when fear of conflict came into play. The younger soldiers we were working with had never been in a live combat situation before. They thought they were just going to show up with their gear and stroll through the city without being hassled. Not only were we potentially fired upon, but we had to hold our response and think clearly in the middle of the action.

The shooter in the hotel had been aiming at us. One of our snipers took him out the next time he leveled a missile. On the ground, our team didn't have to react. We had to focus on getting our civilians out of the combat zone. We had advanced teams building sandbag shelters ahead of us so we could hop from shelter to shelter like a high stakes game of frogger. So, imagine the level of communication that is constantly going on, second by second, to make sure no one screws up.

In the military, lack of decisive action can lead to tragedy. Conflicts can drag on, causing thousands more casualties; leaders can put in jeopardy—the very people they sought to save. In the boardroom, inaction or fear of conflict can actually exacerbate the underlying tensions. As a team dysfunction, this may be the most dangerous.

LACK OF COMMITMENT

As a leader, you have to be committed to the mission, committed to your people, and committed to the execution. It can be easy to embrace the company tagline, but what I tell a lot of the executives I work with is that, yes, you have to be committed to the organization that you represent. However, you have to have a higher level of commitment to the success of your team because without them, you can't achieve what's expected of you.

If you have eight people on your team and they're all fighting, then you're not accomplishing your mission. Commitment to the organization, the team, and the project means less conflict. While fear of conflict is a team dysfunction, the opposite of fear is not an abundance of conflict. You can't seek out conflict or get mired in it when it comes along. When there is too much conflict and not enough commitment within an organization, it's a miserable existence.

Having difficult conversations is a key component of any managerial position. Without the ability to talk to your team members about what they are doing wrong or how they can improve, no project would ever move forward. Many new leaders have accepted the inevitability of difficult conversations and are comfortable with that task when it presents itself. The trick is to get as much as you can out of each conversation and to provide concrete measures so that your employee can evaluate their own performance.

You need to identify your expectations of your team, yourself, and the product you are creating. That way, when you have a difficult conversation with someone who is not meeting those standards, you can say, "This is our standard." Explain how the employee has failed to meet that standard and ask for their feedback. "Is this something that you don't know how to do? Have we given you the tools and resources to do this, or have you had to figure it out on your own?" The problem may be a training issue. Perhaps you need a more formal or rigorous onboarding process. The problem might be an individual one; maybe that team member doesn't have the drive or the skills necessary. Or maybe they have the skills, but their personality is such that it doesn't gel with the team and creates inauthenticity.

You don't always have to have the problem nailed down to understand that something is not working. This might not be the right place for your employee. If their work doesn't match the standards, then something has to change. You can conduct the conversation without blaming, which will lead to better results than finger pointing and name calling. A typical leader might say, "You're screwing up. You're not doing your job. What's your problem?" It's because they're not focusing on helping their team member or achieving their mission; they're focused on themselves. They're getting chewed out by their boss for not making the numbers. They feel embarrassed and they don't know how to fix it.

That tactic doesn't improve anything. When we talked about Maslow's Hierarchy and psychological safety, we discovered that people need to feel included if they are going to do their best work. You can't innovate if you're afraid for your job. That isn't to say there aren't some problem employees that may need a metaphorical kick in the pants. But any conversation should always be tied to the standards of operation that your company has set. By singling out an individual for disciplinary action without referencing the approved standards, you are setting yourself up for a lawsuit.

Giving the team member the benefit of the doubt, you can go into the difficult conversation by explaining, "Here's why the company is doing what they're doing." Explain why the individual role is so critical. There are two common reasons for mistakes: either the employee doesn't want to do their job, or they don't know how to. When I work with leaders on this subject, I advise them to make the assumption that the individual doesn't know how to, before starting to blow up. Ask the question, "Is this something that you were not taught to do?" Or ask, "Could you walk me through your process with this? Help me understand where you feel uncomfortable with XYZ." Maybe they're not comfortable doing it. Not everyone is a good salesperson, regardless of drive or ambition. This may not be the right position for your struggling team member. Make sure your support is well articulated before asking them to open up about what is wrong. You need all the information you can gather before making a decision that will affect the team, the company, and the individual. Just like being in a hole and wondering where the shot came from, you need all the information to avoid making a disastrous decision.

Sometimes people don't have the training they need, but sometimes all the training in the world just isn't enough. I can teach you how to play basketball, but that doesn't necessarily mean you'll develop the skill to be in the NBA. You could be great in the rec league, but there's a natural component to the game that can't be taught. I hear people say any skill can be taught. Absolutely. But is that skill going to meet the standard required for the entire team to perform at the level expected?

Your job as a leader is to discern what is the best environment in which each team member can naturally thrive.

There are scientific analysis tools specifically designed to help you make those decisions. These tools will tell you the type of environment it takes to thrive, the potential value to the team, and even the preferred natural skills you can expect from each person based on their results. You identify what motivates them, and you do what you need to do as a leader to communicate in order to elevate their natural desire to want to be part of the team.

A lack of commitment will lead team members to go off on their own, to either drop the ball or refuse to pick it up entirely. If you are dealing with a lack of commitment, difficult conversations may be the only way to explore the root cause. When you have determined that a person needs additional support, or that they haven't received appropriate training, you can always explain the company and mission standards and set up an improvement plan to help them.

Be aware that not everyone is going to be a Michael Jordan or a Lebron James. Even with appropriate training, not every team member is going to develop the skills to meet the standards that you have set. In that case, you can turn to repositioning the team member or helping them transition out of the team. Whatever the case, respect your team member and their choices, and try not to focus on your own numbers. This type of dysfunction can drag the entire team down if you are not careful.

COMMUNICATION AND COMMITMENT IN COMBAT

Because of my background and skills, and due to the nature of combat in the early 2000s, a lot of the missions I worked on were similar. It is a common thing for teams deployed in different theaters of operations around the world to have confusion on the battlefield. You don't always know whether incoming fire is friendly, mistaken, or actually designed to kill you. For that reason, communication, traning, discipline, and commitment are key factors to achieving your mission and getting out alive.

This story began like many others. We were providing cover for diplomats attempting to flee from an embassy under fire. It was the dead of night; we were surrounded by desert. My Marine detachment was working with the Navy to set up a perimeter in front of the hotel where the enemy combatants were lodged. Imagine massive equipment in dunes of sand, explosions going off left and right, and us in the middle of it trying to escort civilians to safety.

Any decision we made had to be coordinated with everyone else. The Navy with their crafts, the SEAL team snipers at both ends of the line, and all the leaders and teams on the ground had to be in sync in order to accomplish the mission. So, the leaders were taking a step back to observe the entire line and communicate with each other. Every word has to be clear, and there can be no ambiguity. A split second is all it takes for people to wind up dead. These are the rules of engagement Marines live by; these are the standards used to measure effectiveness when lives are on the line.

I heard a shot that I thought was coming at us. The natural tendency is to react in that type of charged environment, to fire back at whoever is firing at you. But we were trained to observe and wait for information, to stay engaged and focused on the mission. If you give in to your survival instincts and react with deadly force, you could put the whole team at risk. The more communication you have, the more certainty of action.

Commitment to the mission has to override your first instinct. If there is no commitment, your team will be just a group of people acting in their own self-interest. Lack of cohesion can have dramatic effects both on and off the battlefield. Your customers or the civilians you are escorting to safety must be able to trust you to deliver on your promises. When your team suffers from a lack of communication and discipline instilled by traning and commitment, those promises may never be fulfilled.

AVOIDANCE OF ACCOUNTABILITY

If a team understands what needs to be done and they're working together, they're going to hold each other accountable because there's pride created by the standards they measure themselves by. They have trust in each other, they are willing to have challenging conversations, and are committed to each other and the mission. There are grounds to both work well with each other and, above all, to hold each other to higher standards. There's a sense of performance. Each team member has a stake in the outcome and wants to ensure that the mission or the project is completed. In a high-performing team, people understand the goal and their own responsibilities in relation to that goal. The focus is the mission, something greater than themselves and has a positive effect once accomplished. No one drops the ball because everyone knows where they need to be and when. Commitment creates a sense of responsibility for how each job affects the ability of someone on their team to do theirs. Each action, like a chain, is interconnected. There's a sense of what the deadlines are, what the chain of command looks like, and how a finished product will be evaluated. In a dysfunctional team, people don't know what is expected of them. They view the distribution of labor as unfair or arbitrary and they avoid accountability for their failures.

Most ineffective leaders fail to assign roles based on strength. Team members can come to you from a variety of places. Maybe some you hired, but others were transferred from different departments. Maybe you're stepping into a team that has already been created, and you are left to discover each person's strengths and weaknesses on your own. You want to make sure each person is comfortable with their assignment and has the necessary skills and experience to execute your vision. The more clearly you can define their individual end goals and how their contribution helps to achieve that goal, the better the results will be. Once everyone understands their responsibilities, the desire to avoid accountability is replaced by hard work. People want to see their team succeed and to be a part of that success.

Everyone either wants to be in charge or they want to be measured by their individual results. In business as in the military, you are often judged as a team. Whether the mission is completed or the product launched, depends on how you work together, not on any one individual. If the team shines, then everyone is rewarded. If the team fails, then it is time to reevaluate the dynamics.

As a next generation leader, you have more influence than you think you do. You set the tone for the team culture and model appropriate behavior; if you blame others for shoddy work instead of focusing on the problem, your team will do the same. If you reward employees strictly for sales numbers, and not customer longevity or value, they will read into that too. Cultural Key Performance Indicators (KPIs) must be addressed as well, and within this metric, you must be able to determine how well an employee adapts to the team and whether he can thrive or not in your corporate environment. At some point, most people will revert to self-preservation and psychological safety. But if the culture is about team dynamics as a whole, then you can eliminate the silos and encourage everyone to accept responsibility.

TEAMWORK AND ACCOUNTABILITY IN THE MARINES

Sometimes the command structure is clear, as with organizational charts and hierarchies. Sometimes it is flat, as with collaborative work cultures and newer environments. The military understands the value of each and creates a time and a place for changing accountabilities. As a leader, I quickly learned that I did not have to know everything. I did not have to be the one doing everything because then my team would ostracize me. A leader who can't delegate is seen as a micromanager. No one person can be an expert in everything, and even with an inordinate amount of skill, it is impossible for one individual to be in ten places at once.

The leader's job is to identify the natural skills of each member of the team. And depending on the mission, the person suited to lead changes. In one operation, I rotated my team through four different leaders. Each person had the specific skills to command the troops during their function. My job at that time was to make sure that everyone did their individual job to accomplish the specific mission.

The objective was simple, but the execution would be very complex. We were dispatched to take out a radio tower in a not-so-good neighborhood in a foreign country that we were not on the best diplomatic terms with. To accomplish our goal, we had four different objectives. One, we had to get onto the beach undetected. Two, we had to navigate the town. Three, we had to get to the tower, destroy it, and, finally, we had to have an exit. So that meant I needed a demo expert and a navigational expert. I needed someone who understood the cultural aspects of the foreign town, so we could dress and act in an appropriate fashion and not stand out. We also had to have someone who understood the topography. It would be easy to get trapped if we didn't understand the landscape, so we needed someone local to give us that information.

My very first point man was the person who understood the village. They were in charge of navigating us through the landing, to the village, and through the village to the tower. We had to find transportation because we couldn't walk as a group of outsiders. We landed at night. And we took back roads. But it was a small town, so as soon as anyone saw anything, everyone was going to know.

Just because you have an asset, or a person from the village who is helping you out, doesn't mean you trust them. They could have all sorts of motivations for bringing you into the town. The person on my team who had made the connection, I trusted them. They had to work the asset to get the information and get us where we needed to be. We dressed in loose clothing, to blend in, and moved in pairs. We went up the harder side of the mountain to avoid the more populated route, but still had to avoid goat herders. There were a few scouts who went ahead to radio back information. It took a long time to get to the tower, and for the entire journey, we were relying on these scouts, and the people who were handling the local assets.

Once we got to the tower, the demo expert took charge. In a seamless transition, the team focused on his needs and took his instructions to make sure the demolition happened in a timely fashion. As the expert was setting the explosives, we took a supportive role and provided security so he could focus on his job without worrying about anything else. After the explosives were set, someone else took the lead to get us out of there. I was making sure that all the pieces were doing what they were supposed to, and everyone was staying focused on their job. Not only was the overall mission taking out the tower, but my mission was getting my people back safely.

Once the tower blew up, everyone knew we were there. Stealth wasn't an option anymore, but that didn't mean I was willing to leave anyone behind. All along, I had to consider the ripple effect of every decision. Was a choice we made in the beginning going to jeopardize our exit? I wasn't the one in charge of each mission component, but I was responsible for seeing the entire team work together to accomplish our goal. No plan survives the battlefield. You've still got to have that big picture view of the operation.

Each expert was accountable for their own process, and the team transitioned from one team leader to the next based on the skill set involved. As the team leader, I was accountable for ensuring that the operation transitioned from one stage to the next and that each of my team members had what they needed to execute their job perfectly. I had to smooth over the transitions, think on my feet, pivot if we needed to, and bring each team member to a place where they could perform their task.

INATTENTION TO RESULTS

The final dysfunction is inattention to results. People get so caught up in the daily grind that they forget to even pay attention to the outcome. Many new leaders are focused on their own status, their egos, and the numbers. But that is not the same thing as focusing on results. Poor leaders only think of themselves going up Maslow's Hierarchy of needs. They achieve security for themselves, they achieve belonging through saying the right things to the right people, but they fail to bring their teams along. They create toxic work environments by focusing only on their own needs and ignoring their team members, colleagues, and projects.

You can tell when someone is truly confident, because through their actions, they allow others to be confident in themselves. It is contagious when done right. True leaders are confident enough to say, "I want to help you someday have my job." Because they believe they will be going on to bigger and better things, they don't need to squat in the same position for multiple years. They will train you to do what you need to do so that the company and the team can prosper.

People who are faking it will try to make you smaller, so they always have the spotlight. Effective leaders are not afraid to give the spotlight away. Who needs the spotlight when the mission is the focus when the results speak for themselves? Fake leaders are more afraid of losing their ego because they are not confident, and their attention is misplaced. A high-performing team lead by a strong manager will focus on the outcomes and align their work to the goals and to their team's natural strength.

As a next generation leader, help your team concentrate on their individual piece of the puzzle, so that you can achieve your outcome as a group. What does each person need to get from where they are to where you see they could be? How can you support that? And it's amazing how it's reciprocated. When your team feels that you've got their back, they'll let go of all that anxiety and stress that is holding them back. They'll do whatever they have to do and go to hell for you. This only happens when there is trust, vulnerability, commitment, communication, accountability, and focus.

I've sat down with executives and CEOs. I said, "If I were to ask you to give me the names of your top performers, could you do it?"

Undoubtedly, they say, "Yes." Boom, boom, boom. They list the names of the people that come through for them often.

Then I say, "Give me the names of the ones that are in the middle." They struggle. If I ask for the names of the ones who are just brand new, very rarely can anyone answer. You need to know all of your team members, and if some of them are struggling, you need to know what motivates them, why they are there, and what drives them.

How often have you sat down with your top performers and simply asked them the question, "What drives you to be here every day?" Most managers look at me like, *what do you mean?* I say, "I don't mean a five− or a ten-year plan. I mean, in the next thirty days, why are you here? What is it you're having to do and achieve and accomplish for the next thirty days? Is it a mortgage or car payment, a new house you bought, or are you going to have a baby? Are you saving for college or a vacation?" These are real motivations that are somehow lost in the performance metrics but are often just as important to your team members as that next promotion.

Once you uncover their immediate motivation, you can help each team member develop a plan to get them there. This exercise will prove to your employees that you are in touch with their real lives. You understand that it is not all about work, but what work can do for their families and their futures. You can bridge the gap between work life and home life and encourage them to give you their best. You can have these conversations not only with your top performers, but also with people who are struggling in the middle. A scheduled half hour of undivided attention will pay dividends.

When you have these conversations, it is no longer about you anymore. The team can focus on their project or their mission, now that they know their job is safe. It's about moving them up that hierarchy of needs. Only at the top of the pyramid are you going to see real innovation, creativity, and risk-taking that is necessary for true success.

At the core of every infrastructure team performance issue is communication, either the lack thereof or the conflicting part of it. Once I bring groups together and clearly define the goals and the standards, not only do they realize they want the same things, but they come to understand what is holding them back. They learn how, together, they can fix what is broken and how to improve on the next steps.

Each person arrives at the same conversation with a different lens that filters words and actions through past experiences. Part of communication is understanding that your own assumptions and common sense are unique to you and not to the other person. Once you recognize your own filters, you can do your best to set them aside and really listen to your employee. It is the only way to remain open to all results, rather than just the ones you want to see. Steven Covey once said, "We all speak the same language but use a different dictionary."

Inattention to results can mean ignoring poor results in favor of better indicators. It can also mean glossing over achievements made by other people or claiming those achievements for yourself. A true leader brings their team to victory and shares the spotlight with everyone involved. Imagine if you were coaching a basketball team instead of leading a department. If you failed to win the championship but had two of the top ten most improved players in your ranks, that is something to celebrate. That stat reflects well on you as the coach, on your team members who won the award, and also for the team members who didn't. You have to pay attention to all the results, not just the ones everyone is talking about.

INATTENTION TO RESULTS IN THE CORPORATE WORLD

The casino that I worked with to help them break out of a cycle of plummeting sales was inattentive to the results of their sales campaign. The competition was eating into the marketplace. This particular casino owned the strip as far as events that had the most square footage. They were the most technologically savvy, but they were also known as the hardest to deal with. The VP had created a culture of fear, where everyone's job was on the line. They had very talented people who were stuck in the safety phase of Maslow's Hierarchy.

During the training, as I was explaining what drives people, I stumbled upon the answer. They were trying to incentivize their salespeople with bonuses, but they were narrowing everything down to numbers and making people too nervous to achieve those bonuses. For example, they had a computer tracking system that they plugged everything into. It told you whether that percentage was accepted or not as far as profit margin. Salespeople were spending inordinate amounts of time and energy tracking their progress on this global system. And all the bonus and retention decisions were based on this one piece of equipment. The reason the competitors were winning over their market wasn't the numbers; it was because they were more relational. So, the casino hired me to come in and train their salespeople to be more relational.

I brought up the Maslow's Hierarchy, not only as it relates to the client's psychological safety and belonging, but the sales team's as well. The moment people feel that their job is on the line, it introduces a transactional element. To combat that, you need to change the culture of the workplace. You can start to incentivize the depth of the client relationship. What is the level of trust that is established?

The casino had a team whose job it was to infiltrate into these big corporate elements and win their business. It would take them six months on average to woo a six-figure client and successfully land an event. Once that happened, once the salesperson had closed the deal, the casino would take the client from them and give it to somebody else on a different team.

When I heard about this, I asked, "How many times does that happen?" I put it on a whiteboard. "You got one event from each of these twenty-five major clients. How often do you get a second or third event?" And it went from twenty-five clients to three. I said, "Based on these results, why do you transfer the client?"

"Because now they're internal," they explained. "It's a different department that is in charge of internal clients."

I thought about that. "Okay. The responsibilities don't need to change. You can still treat the internal client differently from the prospective client. But when you take away the relationship builder, then it becomes a transaction, rather than a relationship. You are losing the majority of your customers after only one event. How do you think that affects your bottom line?"

Seeing that the sales team was frustrated, I went on. "Here's what I want you to do for the next six months. The sales team that brought them on board will get a percentage from the initial event. And then they will bring in a smaller percentage for every subsequent event, but don't transfer the relationship.

You can transfer the role, have the internal customer service team working behind the scenes, but keep the relationship builder as the point of contact for the client. So that person who brought the customer to the dance, will still be going home with them." They went from losing seventy-five percent of their initial business to gaining almost eighty-five percent of those secondary events just by making that one small change.

DYSFUNCTION COMES IN ALL COLORS

The five common dysfunctions of a team can be seen in corporate America as well as on the battlefield, in sports teams, and families. I once worked with a European company that manufactured all of the machines for bottling companies, the conveyer belts, and stuff like that. These things are massive, and they all have to be built in sections.

The floor was painted to indicate where one process ended and the next one began. It was like a flow chart written onto the actual factory floor. When each component was finished, it was moved to the next section where there was a whiteboard. And that whiteboard had a list of components and processes to tell each engineer what they were doing. Next to each description was a red, yellow, or green light. If the process or component was completed with no problems, it was coded with a green light. If there were minor complications, the process would receive a yellow light. And if something had to be fixed before it could move on, it would get a red light because that would affect the timing of the next section.

As people walked by, they could see at a glance where each section was. And if it was yellow or red, action was taken instantly, no discussion needed. Whether you develop a visual chart of your own, or merely take the temperature of the room at regular intervals, communication is key. If you have that constant contact and you have that deeper layer of insight, you can mine for conflict quicker and address it while it's still a small issue. But the leader has to set that tone. You have to have trust and vulnerability. People need to be open to conflict and able to move past it, rather than avoiding and deflecting. Commitment and accountability are vital to success and when you achieve results, whatever they may be, you need to pay attention.

One of your many jobs as a new team leader is to help your people navigate the minefield of the typical dysfunctions. Any one of the pitfalls can bring your productivity to a halt, as well as cause your numbers to plummet and team members to start looking for other jobs. Using a combination of respect and communication, you can help your team focus on their goals. Having a relational approach rather than a transactional one will invigorate your employees, establish new relationships with clients, and help maintain those existing relationships.

SCAN ME
PDF flowchart on how to use the
5 dysfunctions to build a high-performing team

CHAPTER 9:

CONNECTING THE DOTS

COMMUNICATION IS MORE DIFFICULT THAN IT SEEMS

Have you ever had an experience where you think you communicated effectively, but your employee still has questions? Or maybe you thought you told your friend to pick you up at the airport at three, but they arrived at two and waited at the wrong terminal? Every conversation goes through filters in the brain.

THE COMMUNICATION PROCESS

INTENDED MESSAGE ⟶ RECEIVED MESSAGE
RECEIVED MESSAGE ⟵ GAP ⟶ INTENDED MESSAGE

COMMUNICATION FILTERS
- Personality
- Language
- Culture
- Time
- Perception
- Interest
- Experience
- Emotions
- Internal distractions
- Message design
- Communication channel

The person listening hears the words through a filter that has been created long before that specific conversation. They may hear different words altogether based on their own unique filter. For example, your friend who was supposed to pick you up at three p.m., had just been to the airport to pick up her mother at two p.m. the week before. Without stopping to consider your details, she agreed to pick you up and went to the same meeting location and time as her previous appointment. Before a communication gets to the rational part of someone's brain, it passes through layers of baggage and noise.

These filters are based on experience, upbringing, IQ, and all the things our mammalian brain is focused on. A listener will pick a message apart to discover what's the most relevant as far as safety and security are concerned. They will compare what you said to past experiences to see if there is a match. Whatever seems relevant based on those two objectives is reacted to first. Only later, if ever, does the listener consider other components of the communication. That is how a person understands what you just said.

When we are texting or in a digital communication, certain clues are missing. We have to interpret intent from the written word, instead of body clues or tone of voice. If you are mad and someone sends you a text, you will read that text through that mad filter. Even though the intent of the message was not negative. If that person's insecure and you're a leader and you're trying to get that person to do something, they're going to read your words through an insecure filter. "Oh my God," they might say. "He doesn't trust me. He doesn't have confidence in me." No matter what you have said, they interpret your words this way because that's their lens of insecurity. As a leader, you have to be aware of this tendency and do what you can to mitigate it. If you don't build up your team's confidence, then they will never hear your words as you meant them to be heard. You will never get through the way you want to.

As leaders, you have to address each person from their perspective in that moment and understand what you need to say to them to get the response necessary. What do they need? What is their motivation? That's where vulnerability comes into play. If you have established an honest workplace, then they can communicate their anxieties to you. If they're insecure, find out what's causing that insecurity. Maybe they are in a room full of top performers, and they don't know if they can compete.

It's amazing when you start to open those lines of communication, and you can see a human being instead of just a collection of animal responses. We evolved for ten million years, only the last few thousand in developed societies. There is a lot going on under the surface of every conversation that has nothing to do with words. People go straight to concerns about survival, creating uncomfortable situations. If you can identify what filter is being used, then you can address those assumptions and move towards a better understanding. If you don't clearly change that filter, you will always get the same result.

BUT WE ALL SPEAK ENGLISH, RIGHT?

We may all speak English, but we don't all use the same dictionary. Even though everyone here in the U.S. speaks English, that does not necessarily mean we can understand each other. For example, if you took a person born and bred in Boston and dropped him in the middle of the bayou in New Orleans, he might have a difficult time communicating with the locals, not to mention avoiding the alligators. The pace or speed of how the locals speak and the dialect they use are unfamiliar to him. The same might happen if you took a surfer from California and dropped him in the middle of the Bronx. He might find it challenging and may even be in shock. Duuuude!

As we mentioned in Chapter 3, some people move at a faster pace; they act before they think, tend to be more aggressive, always seem to be on the go, and are likely to be outspoken. On the other side of the spectrum in the reserved area, people tend to move at a slower pace; the term slower pace does not refer to their intelligence level or capabilities, simply the rhythm or speed in which they tend to think and move. This group tends to process and think before they act, they want facts and information, and they seem quiet and reserved.

- Where are you more comfortable fifty-one percent of the time?
- Do you tend to be faster paced or slower paced?
- Where does each person on your team fall in the map?

What we have found through our research is that connection starts here. It is also where most communication misfires happen. If you are a slower-paced leader in a conversation with a fast-paced employee and they are talking to you at a million miles per hour and trying to convince you of something, you might become a little irritated.

- Would you follow someone who irritates you?

- Can you do business with people who are irritated?

Most of the time, we are not aware of this difference because this is who we are naturally. That is why it is important to discover where we stand in the connection phase and adapt to who we are speaking to and allow them to be comfortable, so they can engage and focus on what we are saying. Can communication be engaging without a connection? In my experience, it cannot.

In the military, our life depends on reaction, not hesitation. We were expected to be of the same mind and movement with instant obedience to order. This was achieved through intense training and physical and mental endurance, while a drill instructor yelled in our ears to push harder.

This, however, did not translate well into the civilian mindset. Imagine a tennis mom with three kids, a dog, and a minivan trying to lose ten pounds. I was her personal trainer, screaming in her face to "Give me 10 more!" and "Stop whining!" It did not have the same effect as it did with my recruits. Needless to say, she did not return after our initial session. (I think she may still be in therapy.)

It was not until later that I learned to connect with my clients in *their language* in order to motivate them and eventually see results. This, in turn, increased my business, my quality leads, and, above all, my profits. I took this lesson and applied it to my teams. I asked myself, *How would I speak to my employees if they were my clients?*

Being intense can cause a more reserved or slower paced client to think you are in need of decaf or, even worse, anger management. But being too laid back may irritate some employees who wish you would *"JUST GET TO THE POINT ALREADY!"* We all act and speak from our own common language or the **perception** in which we give the most priority to in that moment and in that environment. As with breathing or blinking, we don't think about it, we just do it. We need to reframe our perceptions and begin to see the needs of our team members from their vantage point. Then we can provide them with the solutions they are looking for which, in turn, will create a comfort zone and an experience they will enjoy and thrive in. This is where performance increases.

It is just like being in that foreign country. After a week of struggling to communicate, you find a store owner who speaks your language, enough for you to understand each other. At that moment, you may feel relief that someone understands you and can finally assist you with your needs, which improves your experience and your comfort zone. It allows you to like and trust that person and creates a memorable moment you won't forget and will likely share with others.

HUMAN NEEDS IN COMMUNICATION

Every human being has a primary and secondary need. For example, some people have a primary need for intelligence. They want to feel smart. That becomes one of the filters they see the world through. Every conversation becomes about intelligence—theirs and other people's. If they are feeling confident within that need, they will be able to react much more appropriately. If they are feeling anxiety because they're not getting those needs met, they will react out of a place of insecurity. They might worry about whether they seem smart and obsess about people's opinions.

Imagine you're brand new to a team and you're trying really hard to be well received. It's actually a chemical reaction in our brain; these needs are our drugs. When we are in an anxiety situation, our brain reacts as if it is not getting the drug it is addicted to. It says, "I'm not getting significance" or "I'm not getting intelligence feedback that I'm looking for." Anxiety goes up. You become an addict. You need it. We take these desires to a whole new level.

When leaders understand this and say, "Okay, this person's primary need is for me to recognize his intelligence," then they can have that conversation with the new employee. "Hey, I know you're new here. We're going to walk you through this process. The reason I hired you was because I know you can make an impact on this team. The rest of the team doesn't realize it yet because you're going to be the smartest person on this team. Once we're all said and done, I need your smarts to create the process. Not only to perform, but also create an impact." If you say those things, it will be the equivalent of giving the employee a shot of the drug they're craving.

Once an individual has moved up a level in Maslow's Hierarchy and they are comfortable having their basic needs met, they will develop a secondary and possibly a tertiary need. There are always two predominate ones. For example, they might need intelligence acknowledgement and then belonging. They want to be a part of the team culture, not just a part of the process.

These needs are not well hidden. As a manager, you should be able to discover what your team members are hungry for after a few conversations. By giving them the acknowledgement in the exact target area they need, you can motivate them to do their best.

BAMCIS

Communication is the focus of this book because it helps facilitate every process. By listening to what your employees and customers are saying, you can establish a trusting, productive environment. However, there are skills needed for leadership beyond communication.

BAMCIS (pronounced "bam-sis") is an acronym for: Begin planning, Arrange for reconnaissance, Make reconnaissance, Complete the plan, Issue the order, and Supervise. It is a core tenet of Marine Corps leadership. The goal is to gather information, make a plan, execute, and ensure the success of the mission.

BAMCIS is used to describe the time-tested steps used by Marines to enable a logical and orderly process for making the best use of time, facilities, and personnel when preparing and executing a mission. It is a way to move beyond conversations and execute your plan. It can be helpful in business as well as in the military to ensure a comprehensive battle strategy and a winning process. BAMCIS stands for:

- B – Begin the Planning
- A – Arrange for Reconnaissance – Gather information.

- M – Make Reconnaissance – Do research, team planning, and define key milestones.
- C – Complete the Planning – Bring the research, team skill, and desired outcomes together to create the plan of action.
- I – Issue the Order – Based on skill and ability, assign responsibility and deadlines.
- S – Supervise – Observe and manage when needed to make sure all is going according to plan. When something goes wrong, guide – don't take over – to course correct.

I focus on listening and communication because those skills are often missing from traditional leadership training. While you need to foster your team's productivity through honest conversation, you also need to execute flawlessly. BAMCIS can provide a roadmap for taking your project from brainstorming to implementation. It is a component of leadership that can't be ignored.

MASLOW'S HIERARCHY AND THE FIVE DYSFUNCTIONS

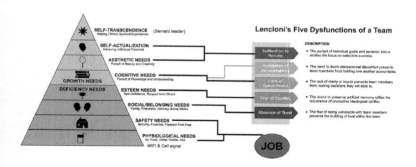

A lot of these human behavioral theories are connected in ways that the original theorists didn't anticipate. For example, Maslow's Hierarchy of Needs is directly correlated with Lencioni's Five Dysfunctions of a Team. When individual needs are not being met, people revert to more basic levels of functioning. The team dysfunctions become more common.

I have developed a model to show how each of the dysfunctions relate to unmet needs. If social/belonging needs are not met, there is an absence of trust. If esteem needs are not met, there is fear of conflict. When cognitive needs are not met, the result is lack of commitment and avoidance of accountability. At the top of the charts, a lack of self-actualization and aesthetic needs prompt inattention to results.

My best example of Maslow's needs being unmet is in the casino whose leader threatened the jobs of all of her salespeople. That action immediately sent the entire staff to the bottom of Maslow's Hierarchy, where they were afraid for their basic safety. As a result, every major team dysfunction was in evidence.

While I one hundred percent advocate for making employees feel safe on the job, I do understand there are times when an individual doesn't belong on a certain team or interferes with productivity. In that case, there may be a need for a difficult conversation. Keeping the problem employee's basic needs in mind will help your communication. Honesty will encourage trust and, with any luck, you can move the person to a better suited situation. That process is entirely different than a blanket statement that not hitting sales targets will result in termination. If you want the best from your people, you have to give them the best from yourself.

CONNECTING THE DOTS

Now that we know there are intersections between different behavioral theories, we can combine them in such a way that will boost productivity for your team. You can use Maslow's Hierarchy and Lencioni's Five Dysfunctions of a Team to further understand the concepts of growth versus defensive mindset and how the mammalian brain overcomes the filters that affect how you really communicate with your employees. Once you establish open communications and give the employees what they need, you can use BAMCIS to attack your projects. Having both a plan for execution and the ability to listen to your team members will elevate you beyond other managers in your company. It will put you in a position to make a real difference.

CHAPTER 10:

FINISHING THE PUZZLE

FORMULA FOR PEAK PERFORMANCE

In my consulting business, I create milestones for participants. The first and most critical is for them to *listen* and be willing to hear new ideas from their team members. The assignment is to listen and to respond appropriately. For example, say, "This is what I heard," and repeat the team member's idea back to them, making sure you understand the details. You must find common ground, to implement your ideas and their ideas (where it makes sense).

Afterwards, I have team members evaluate their new leader. At the end of the week, I talk to everyone who has come to the participant with new ideas. They evaluate themselves, and then we have a conversation to see how they have improved. That way we can create a self-analysis that has traction, and I can develop something around that to help them improve. Those who are serious can use the assessment for discovery. They have a group of people to hold them accountable, but there's also a process that helps them understand if they're improving.

One of my mentors, who introduced me to this technique, said, "If you want to impact a million people, you have to start by impacting one person." If you're struggling to improve yourself, but you are focused on the next best thing, how can you possibly get there? The greater the quality of your presentation, the greater the confidence that you have, the more you are going to be able to affect the world. Just like a sound wave, or like a wave in the water when it expands, it keeps losing that intensity. You have to start with something big and bold in order to impact millions of people down the line.

If that's your end game, you'll need a formula for peak performance. It starts with listening and communication. Never be afraid to learn more. By evaluating yourself and honing your skills, you will extend your reach and your ability to manage better, more productive teams. Using BAMCIS, you can build a game plan, and by understanding behavioral theory you put yourself in a good position to get your message across. If you want to impact a million people, you have to start by impacting one, yourself. By improving yourself and your communication abilities, you will be able to affect change in the world around you.

GROWTH AND PRODUCTIVITY

A pain point is something that causes growth. People don't like pain, and it becomes an incentive to change. Growth and productivity are two ways out of pain, and things that every business wants to encourage.

The four components around growth that made a huge impact are: high productivity, personality, individuality, and clear direction. These are four qualities that we look for in an effective leader and are basic indicators of future success. Another factor that tends to have a lot of weight is vision. Vision creates communities and helps rally the troops. Leaders need to have communication skills, the ability to engage employees, and hiring and retaining policies that attract quality people. All of these considerations will affect the growth of a leader, their employees, and the organization.

Productivity focuses more on human capital, specifically around establishing talented, driven teams. You need a complimentary combination of skills and sympathetic personalities to develop a high-performing team. By putting the right people together and supporting them, you will see that productivity goes up in the work environment. Once you have those people, you need to make sure the environment is conducive for the right process.

Another measure of productivity is employee wellness; not just the emotional quotient, but when each employee feels they are part of the equation. Training, onboarding, and continuing education help. You may have someone with the aptitude for design, but who came into your department as an assistant. By developing skills through ongoing opportunities, you can make sure you have the best and the brightest in the right positions. Employees must have motivation, efficiency, and choices if they are to give you their best work.

PUTTING IT INTO PRACTICE

Do you really want to connect with your team as a leader or do you want to be a dictator? Companies run on both sides. You can share the same background as a person like the casino owner, but it's the approach that's unique. Some people will thrive in any environment, but more people will thrive in a supportive environment.

I interviewed all the employees of King-Sized Eats when I worked with the CFO who became COO. I interviewed his bookkeeper and his project managers and asked them to tell me what wasn't so good about him. "If you could snap your fingers and change something about him, what would that be?" I asked. "What is the negative impact to your productivity and your quality of life?"

The team said that he was micromanaging.

I followed up with, "What's the negative impact?"

"I can't help my customers because I have to take everything back to him for approval," someone said. "He isn't open to new ideas."

The negative impact is that they were behind in creativity and innovation. And their competition was now knocking at the door of their clients. There was no clear vision or direction for what they were doing and why they were doing it. A big problem was revealed when employees told me, "I don't know if I have a future."

So, then I asked, "What would you like for him to improve?"

They wanted him to be able to listen to their ideas and where they were coming from. They represented the front where the customers were, and they could hear what the customers were saying. The team wanted him to be more precise as to the vision and why they were doing what they were doing, not just jumping on the new trends or regurgitating buzz words.

They said, "We'd like for him to train us and to give us the knowledge that he has for us to improve, as far as a direction and a career path."

We developed a list of the top three things the staff was looking for. First was training, second was better listening, and third was more precise communication. When we boiled it all down, at the end of the day, there was no confidence in the growth of the business. There was no clarity of vision, mission, or direction. The COO felt the need to prove himself, because he felt he had made so many mistakes that he became gun shy. Feeling like an imposter is such a common problem, that we need to spend a little bit of time discussing that one single anxiety.

IMPOSTER SYNDROME

People need to feel that when they have reached a certain level of accomplishment, they have permission to be in that position. Imposter syndrome is a psychological term that describes people who don't allow themselves that permission. They feel like, even though they have by all rights from the outside world, the credentials or skills to hold their position, that people will somehow find out they are not worthy. They have not met the internal mental matrix of how they measure success. And they sometimes don't even know how to measure success or when they would ever feel like they have "made it." They self-implode.

If you don't have the right mentors or the right value mechanism or clear internal purpose, you are constantly battling yourself. You may have an ivy league degree and you may have brought value to your company, but because of that self-imposed doubt, you can't appreciate what you've earned. We all have this connected definition of success. A sufferer might say, "I don't look like so and so," or "I didn't go through the same thing as this other person that I admire, so how can I be seen as successful?"

That shows integrity and value mechanism. There's a disparity between the perception of the position and how people see themselves. They might become a movie star and all of a sudden, everybody is interested in them. They're like, "Holy crap, how do I deal with this?" They don't see themselves as the outside world sees them. There's that disconnect between the mask that other people put on because of the role or the accomplishment and who they really are behind it. And when there's a big disparity, that's when you see the imposter element.

I knew this happened with celebrities, but I didn't realize it was so pervasive in the CEO world. I taught a couple of my courses and participants said, "Yeah, we have these issues." If they just build a $500 million company over twenty years or even five years, they don't see themselves as the rest of the world sees them. Subconsciously, they have this measuring stick. The world says, "Hey, you have arrived." But in their minds, they are telling themselves, "I don't feel right. I haven't earned the right to be here."

The other thing I noticed after having conversations with many people who suffer from imposter syndrome is that they are all really talented individuals. They do things naturally that most other people can't do. That clicked for me when I wrote my first book. I asked myself, "Who the hell is going to want to read anything about me? Who the hell am I?" It took five years of customers, my wife, and other people telling me, "You do something unique and different than anyone else does. You see things differently." I've had colonels from the military and CEOs in one training.

I did a training for Cox Communications on leadership called *The Marine's Guide to Leadership*. It was fifteen or twenty minutes, nothing major. It was about behavior and our assessment and things of that nature. Both the Colonel and the CEO came up to me and they said, "We've been to thousands of this type of trainings, but the way you presented it was phenomenal. I've never seen anything like it." Even with that type of positive feedback, it's hard to break through that assumption that somehow you haven't earned your success.

SELF-DISCOVERY

Whenever I go into an executive team and we do the assessments, the self-discovery blows everyone away. They can recognize behavioral patterns within themselves, saying,

"Oh, that's why I do this," or, "That's why this person reacts this way when I say that." They can see what they need to do personally to be a better leader. The assessments give them the playbook or the instruction manual for their employees. Using behavioral theory to listen and communicate better, they can recognize what they are doing wrong. That self-discovery is critical.

SCAN ME : GIFT
Tailored report on how to
improve how other people perceive you

BAMCIS is related to self-discovery. At the beginning stage, the planning involves asking questions such as: Who am I? What are my challenges? How am I being perceived? The next step is reconnaissance. You can do a 360-degree survey or get the top five people that know you really well and ask them these questions for self-discovery. After you've collected the data, now there's a game plan for you to improve in several areas. Supervise is the next step in the BAMCIS process. Who will be your accountability partner? Sometimes people come into the process knowing their shortcomings. At least they have an idea that they are doing something wrong and want to fix it.

The CFO of King-Sized Eats was really good with the analytics of technology but could also sell. He was a great people person. So, there was this conflict within him all the time. He finally came to me and said, "You know, I'm losing good quality people. I want to keep building my business. I want to have that customer service mindset. I don't know what I'm doing wrong."

"Okay," I said. "We can go on down this journey, but you have to make this decision. You're going to have to be open to creative and honest criticism from your team. And you have to be disciplined to follow a process." It is all about self-improvement and self-discovery. And I gave him the assessment. Part of it was the interviews with his staff, but part of it was also the self-assessment. I give him credit for being willing to make changes; some people find it too painful to accept criticism and choose to remain stuck in places that don't work.

HOW TO EXECUTE WITHOUT BURNOUT

This is one of the things I do with both veterans and CEOs. I ask for eighteen things that are unique to you. Not things that other people think are special about you, but eighteen things that are unique and quantifiable. And we start to list those things out. Now the secret is because of the imposter syndrome, people don't often take an objective look at their accomplishments. For each unique quality, I ask: Who did that impact? Who did that help? Who did that improve? And how did that lead to this next thing?

Our minds forget a lot of things that we have to be reminded of. Writing it down can show us how many people we have helped or how many projects we have completed. People who have high integrity will say that they're humble. Number one, they don't want to present themselves in an egotistical way. But this exercise is not for the public. You owe it to your customer, that you want to make an impact on, to understand what you've accomplished and find the confidence in yourself that will help you make a better product. Not for you, but for them. If you are functioning at a mediocre fifty percent, you're not hurting you, you're hurting them. The moment that light switches on and people recognize that confidence is not an ego play, is the moment that their lives change. If your goal is to impact one million people with your services in a chain reaction, you have to start with yourself.

LEADING BY EXAMPLE

Human beings are social creatures. To organize our relationships, we put people in one of three boxes: friends, enemies, or indifferent. If you are like me, and I sense that you have my best interests in mind, then you are a friend. If you don't take the time to understand my perspective, and all you want to do is tell me what to do, the natural instinct is to see you as an enemy. But if you're neither of those, then you are indifferent. You don't belong and there's no point in even addressing you. So, this is where you see top performers leading the pack and not the leader.

If the leader is viewed by most of the staff as irrelevant, and the top performers are seen as friends, then the office dynamic changes. I've seen it a lot. For example, people who married into their positions, who are the son— or daughter-in-law of the CEO, might be viewed as irrelevant. If you were promoted because you were a top performer, but not a leader, you might need additional training to make the leap from the "indifferent" box to the "friend" category.

New leaders have to justify their positions. So, they utilize their top performers, but still don't know half the crap the top performers do. They become pseudo leaders where they are just a leader by title. People who are comfortable in this role are too busy protecting the fraud they have created so that they are not exposed. This is why they belittle everybody.

True leaders who have personal confidence actually share that confidence with their team members. They help individuals to grow and even train them to take over their position. They understand that everyone wants to advance, and they don't plan to camp out in their current office. They're great listeners, not because they're trying to manipulate, but because they're trying to understand how to help their employees make it to the next level.

That is one thing we learned from MLK: great leaders empower other leaders. If someone is really engaged when you are talking about things that are important to you, there's an instant connection there. As leaders, it's about listening to what's important to that person to help them achieve those goals and to elevate them. Ineffective leaders use communication skills to manipulate others and grow their position. When you lead by example, elevate, don't manipulate.

CONCLUSION

Every problem we solve, every challenge that we have, starts with either lack of communication or lack of understanding. There is a nationwide inability to communicate, but also misconceptions about the strategy to communicate effectively. That's why listening is a critical tool.

Todays' senior leaders must be able to meet the next generation leaders where they are without stepping on their value system. In 2025, sixty percent of the senior leaders of corporate America will be composed of next generation individuals. Millennials and Xennials must be trained as early as now. Why is this urgent? Because the speed of succession is much faster than it was before the internet. Some older leaders tend to be threatened by next generation leaders because they're afraid to be exposed as not suited for their role or they're afraid that the spotlight will be taken away from them. A true leader must not be threatened.

Older leaders typically have the wisdom while the next generation is more equipped with the technical know-how.

There is a time and a place for each, and if you can work intergenerationally, you will have the best of both worlds.

Performance can be defined in one of three ways, by metrics such as ROI, sales volume, or by relationships and return customers. By locking your company into performance metrics, you are creating a transactional environment. Team members will not be motivated to do their best because their evaluation comes down to only one or two elements. By casting a bigger net, you can encourage your team to function in a more relational way. Relationships are key because every business deals with people. No matter how big a part automation plays, or how large your company has grown, having solid relationships with customers and employees will improve your bottom line.

Every business grows through seven distinct stages as they acquire more employees. Regardless of the type of company or the industry, everyone will have to deal with the same issues. There is chaos in stage one, and a need for well-defined goals and visions in stages three and four. Once you reach the optimal number of employees, your company will change from a "family" feel environment to a "corporate" one. To mitigate this tendency, you can ensure that no team goes above forty-five members.

No matter what you do in business, it is always personal. I have worked with numerous organizations to help them relate to their customers and their employees better. If you try to treat business as separate from the relationships, you will fail. As I saw with the well-established casino, once they removed the point of contact for new events, their sales plummeted. If you take nothing else away from this book, just the understanding that sales are based on relationships would be enough.

Every group goes through The Four Pillars of Adapting™: forming, storming, norming, and performing. Maslow's Hierarchy explains the basic needs people have in order of importance. The Five Dysfunctions of a Team are common ways groups go wrong. Each of these theories was presented by a different social scientist. Each has something to teach us about human behavior. By understanding each theory and how they intersect, we can come away with actionable tools to help us become better leaders.

As a new leader, how can you start to implement some of these tactics:

1. Be curious. Ask questions to better understand your team. What makes them tick, why do they do what they do? Ask their opinion on the direction or strategy you are all working on.

2. Listen to comprehend. It is good to ask questions, however, you have to focus on hearing the answer without prejudice. Be empathetic and genuinely interested in what they are saying. After all, you are the one who asked the questions.

3. Know yourself. Know your strengths, your challenges, your gifts, and your Achilles' heel. Be vulnerable to share and ask for help. Your focus is the team, the results, and the clarity of the vision, not pretending to have a cape and an "S" on your chest.

4. Have clarity of purpose, direction, and outcome. Feel comfortable delegating to those who have a natural ability to accomplish certain tasks and manage the direction and standards of how they do so and how it connects to everyone else.

5. Communicate, communicate, communicate. Common sense only tends to be common to the person speaking. Never assume that everyone sees things the same way you do. Communicate often, get feedback, and match it to your employees' actions to ensure they understood the information. Create safe communication loops so your team feels comfortable sharing ideas, concerns, and struggles at any time. This builds trust and lowers internal firefighting.

6. Engage in continuous education. The more a team works together, learns together, and supports each other, the more effective they become. Find new ways to challenge and increase the acumen for the team as well as improving specific skill sets for each team member. What can you do that will help each person improve their skills both as a team member and as an individual?

7. Finally, start by evaluating the Five Dysfunctions of a Team to see where your team is thriving and where are they lacking. Bring your team together and have a discussion around each definition of the Five Dysfunctions. Create pathways to solve issues and develop standards that will maintain the expectations of quality for the team.

I want to thank you for taking the time to read this information with me. Hopefully, you had a chance to learn the importance of human relations in business. Communication and listening are skills that we all need to practice more. We have to be aware of employees' needs and the filters they use to understand the world. Difficult conversations can be had much easier just by listening to what the employee *isn't* saying. They may be complaining that so and so doesn't hold up their end of the bargain, but what they really mean is they haven't been trained to do the work they are now expected to do.

As a new leader, you can hit the ground running with only a few tools in your belt. Develop a relational environment instead of a transactional one; listen to your team members and be willing to change. After that, you are always welcome to participate in one of the workshops I offer. Click the link below to learn more about the opportunities available.

SCAN ME :
What is next for you?

APPENDIX

INTRODUCTION

James, William. "The Varieties of Religious Experience." *https://www.goodreads.com/author/show/15865.William_James*

"Next Generation Leadership: How to Enhance Performance." Martin Roll. *https://martinroll.com/resources/articles/leadership/next-generation-leadership-how-to-enhance-performance/*

CHAPTER 1

"Recruit Training." *https://www.marines.com/become-a-marine/process-to-join/recruit-training.html*

CHAPTER 2

"The Special Forces of Leadership: Lessons Learned." Leaders. *https://leadersinsport.com/performance/special-forces-1/*

Navarro, Joe. "Be Exceptional: Master the Five Traits That Set Extraordinary People Apart," 2021.

CHAPTER 5

"Growth Mindset – Definition of what it is?" Renaissance. *https://tinyurl.com/edwords.*

CHAPTER 6

"It's Not Nagging: Repetition is Effective Communication." LinkedIn.

Neumeier, Marty. "The Brand Gap: How to Bridge the Distance between Business Strategy and Design," 2003. *https://www.martyneumeier.com/the-brand-gap*

CHAPTER 7

Maslow's Hierarchy of Needs. *https://commons.wikimedia.org/wiki/File:Maslow%27s_Hierarchy_of_Needs.svg*

CHAPTER 8

Lencioni, Patrick. "Five Dysfunctions of a Team," 2000.

"NBA investigating offensive audio recording allegedly by Los Angeles Clippers owner Donald Sterling." *https://www.espn.com/los-angeles/nba/story/_/id/10843525/nba-investigating-offensive-audio-recording-allegedly-los-angeles-clippers-owner-donald-sterling*

Pucker factor. Wikipedia. *https://tinyurl.com/Pucker-factor20.*

Made in the USA
Columbia, SC
05 October 2022

68100227R00130